COSMOGRAPHIA

A POST-LUCRETIAN FAUX MICRO-EPIC

"All Omnia."

– Flann O'Brien

Michael Boughn

BookThug | MMX | Toronto

FIRST EDITION

The production of this book was made possible through the generous assistance of The Canada Council for The Arts and The Ontario Arts Council.

Take what you need and leave the rest.

Some of these poems have appeared previously in the following magazines: *Acta Victoriana, Filling Station, West Coast Line, White Wall, Yellow Edenwald Field.*

Printed in Canada

LIBRARY AND ARCHIVES CANADA CATALOGUING IN PUBLICATION

Boughn, Michael
        Cosmographia : a post-lucretian faux micro-epic /
Michael Boughn.

Poems.
ISBN 978-1-897388-69-3

        I. Title.

PS8553.O834C68 2010   C811'.54   C2010-905583-7

COSMOGRAPHIA

CONTENTS

BOOK I

RAZZAMATOOTIE

"Razzamatootie"
– Dannie Richmond

Canto 1 – Chicken Pie

Surprising voice out of clamour's
jelly roll poultry anthem flags an exact
moment erupting Tootie begins.[1]

How can you say that in Latin
when horns and whistles recall
from before a precise buried today?

Exuberance counters the failure
to shed inflicted syntactical devotion
in place of pies where it goes when

Tootie being the substantive declension
of Razz stumbles out of a previous exile
of insults into the joy of gravy

and thighs, don't forget thighs
flashing through rhymed proliferation
of bang's intimate further hope

That's the Tootie again, intractable[2]
adamant beyond imagination's
admirable reflection of receding bang

big as all git out, further
openings seeming to stutter
of small pies steaming endlessly

When it comes back reclaiming
today, swallows dart through it
still buzzing with Dante's voice

---

[1] "Oh, Lord, I wanna eat that chicken, eat that chicken, eat that chicken
  pie ...." Charles Mingus, Oh Yeah!
[2] "My lady is desired in highest Heaven," Dante, *Vita Nuova, XIX.*

and swart ships, too, light sodden
air alive with bird song
and goat bells figure a pie

morning cannot surpass in other
mornings and songs of raucous
erectile excitements humming

outside the arras knowing
whatever voyeurs lurk in its folds
will never get it especially given

Tootie's refrain to the effect you should
keep your fingers off the clinamen[3]
unless you're ready for the ride

---

[3] Lucretius, *De Rerum Natura,* 2: 216-220.

Canto 2 – Erectile excitements

Helen was another Tootie whose
razz launched some surprising
acts out of Schenectady, bygone
eras massed on the verge chanting
her name till the cows came home

Cows here signify large groups
of meaning headed for the nearest
cliff or store window in the quest
Helen bestowed upon erectile tissues
yearning to come forth in shining borders

Sweet showers still ring with buzz
jigs the works toward whatever pilgrimage
can yet be found beyond dollar day
events in shades of dappled green
out the back door past art's camp

Swell tales of recurrent flow through
old temples now given to tower's
massive investments erected in names
taut with money's tumescent tug
still speak of her tattered glory

starved and secretly barfing
in the bathroom in hope past
participles roaming the stretches of words
might open the secret to her
awkward posture and bleeding wrists

The shop windows unaccountably
extend around former necessity's
shredded and unstrung compositions
into shoddy colonnades of erectile Razz
swelling with dreams of release

That's where Tootie is known to enter
or what H.D. called a Tootie
eidolon,[4] casting its glances hither
and thither with reckless abandon breeding
sprees and spasms wreak havoc

with celestial balance while all along
keeping tumescence in hand though largely
concealed unless needed to bring democracy
to some parched distant land
clamouring for cheap toilet paper.[5]

---

[4] H.D., *Helen in Egypt.*
[5] "[W]e need to accept responsibility for America's unique role in preserving
and extending an international order friendly to our security, our prosperity,
and our principles." "Statement of Principles," Project for a New American
Century.

Canto 3 – Clamour's anthem

The clash you hear may resemble distant
armies if you squint and ignore syntactical

devotion as it rises tall and stiff against
sea's undulating dream of further

earful extensions though even then
similarities breed in withdrawing

roar leaves faith to wander forest
whistling My Jellyroll Soul to distant

ocean proclaiming only to hoot[6]
reasonably matches the quiver

factor as it breaks against kiss
scattering with laws of uncounted

melancholy seeds of yet to be
surprised, unmoored Razz

bearing extreme instances of promiscuous
sounding's miscreant repetitions,

damp intimations, and wine dark
eruptions disturb hope's nagging

insistent claim on laminar nostalgia
afflictions masquerading as cows

---

[6] "Wednesday Night Prayer Meeting," Charles Mingus, *Blues & Roots*.

on their way home. No kiss can get
you past that[7] and even Razz has been known

to throw up hands in gestures signifying
cessation of bovine blundering

while encouraging ambient astonishment's
random misdirections and indiscrete composure

functions to flourish, all indications
of seduction strategies having registered

insignificant successes unworthy
of uncertainty's luminous demand

to face the music and lift your feet
to irregular time function's wiggle insistence.

---

[7] "Ah, love, let us be true / To one another!" Matthew Arnold, "Dover Beach."
See also "Dover Beach," Jack Spicer, *Lament for the Makers*: ". . . No / Baby-
lonian poets employ charms / Each other's arms are not enough either when
the sea shifts and changes / The flight of seagulls here. The pebbles there.
Chickens of some hen."

Canto 4 – Inflicted devotions

There's something to be said

for those silk ropes under the bed
as Susan Sarandon proved unequivocally

with Tim Robbins when he couldn't get
his fast ball magnificent though it was
over the plate though come to think

of it maybe it was leaves of grass
whose syntax John Winthrop no doubt
would have put in the stocks when it
staggered in from the bush smelling

of razzed out bears and the deep funk
of those pendulous boys though *it's*
devotion frankly ups the ante past
pies otherwise friendly game of hold 'em
to be raised and called beyond any reasonable

exhalation advanced devotions measured
in garlands by the pound might be expected
to bring to the table. Beyond that lies
mere poetry, shooting turkeys and holding
forth in uncommon saloons overcoming
yesterday's imposition of bound rudiments

in surprising combinatory beauty
mechanisms.[8] The boggle factor binds
art to shop windows and committee rooms
haggling over expected regulation of public
tootie declensions. It's no place for respectable
intoxicants and random maenads looking

---

[8] "Before even beginning, there is, to my knowledge, no mirror." Victor Cole-
man, "A, The Shepherd whose Voice Never Returns," *MAL ARME, Letter
Drop 3*.

for a dance, the groves hemmed round
with blatant intimations of animal
departures and fleeing forms of errant
critter logic – infliction honks, a signal
to duck or watch your back when they
gather at the river distributing awards
to well crafted iterations of good old pat
on the back for a job well hung
with all those moving devotions

Canto 5 – Joys of gravy

When Tootie howls in an Ellington
mood adrift in the stuff of silk
stockings and curling smoke, Razz
lays down and weeps for all the lost

and broken pies and gravy
deferred. There's nothing, he says
a little animal fat won't make taste
better knowing that's what you've got

to get you through as it feeds
a kind of jubilation oozes
from gashed pies or rises
in song of lush lives lived

in heart of the worst it can
dish out. That's a different gravy[9]
but there's a reason trains
hauling it run into an ease

of transaction within the realm
of many gravies surpassing turbid
ebb and flow in a dance along
strands of unanticipated pebble

logic to break with tracks directional
broadcasts permeating moral
rectumtude's ongoing assaults
on Tootie sorrows and shameless

assertions of erectile excitements
armoured assault on wine dark nests
of terror and palpable instance's

---

[9] "I used to visit all the very gay places / Those come what may places / Where
one relaxes on the axis of the wheel of life," Billy Strayhorn, "Lush Life."

frequent inquisitions regarding
lumpy exterminations and other
interminable interventions
on unanticipated flower responses. Gravy
is as gravy frequently implies

an accessory above and beyond
not to mention within the fact
a veritable bolus appearing *ex nihilo*
naked, too, and yielding no significant

interpretations, no garlands, and no
feasible means of escaping Razz deviations
as they wail and hover rendering
instant's devotions rich, creamy, and meaty.

Canto 6 – Tootie's refrain

Tutti frutti is another guy altogether, he
lives in a different part of town, the houses
in disrepair though by no means squalid
it lacks the spirit of Razz especially
as it becomes Razza'ma of the high
perfect towers and walls that do not
so much keep out as fondle the life
they hold giving it a public shape
in a space of endless pies

It comes down to angle of inclination
implied by Tootie's declension of laminar
strata, a question of kicking a certain
substance into the fan that clicks
away ticking off inconsequential yet
massive formations dwelling
in air infused with the breath
of old spirits murmur within the folds
of moist caverns opening tenuously
to their touch and cascading home

Little Rootie Tootie on the other hand
kicks ass big time, sharing the void
Razz introduces in Epicurean echo
dances to loosen inflicted devotion
arising from too little space
to move, a neutron star like condition
also known as antirazzification[10] to open
all possible temporal calibrations
blowing the time dam with tea for two

---

[10] "To some if you owned your own mind you were indeed sick but when
you possessed an Atonist mind you were healthy. A mind which sought to
interpret the world by using a single loa. Somewhat like filling a milk bottle
with an ocean." Ishmael Reed, *Mumbo Jumbo*.

The concentration of erectile excitements
tips longitudinal celestia into unstable
but firm configurations of toroidal
variance[11] meanwhile leaving displaced
damp paradaisal intimations in compromising
positions to fend for themselves
outside sheets of laminar forbidding
with hardening knowledge of pulse Walt
found in the sea over and over till water
we are laughs and yields its breaking

---

[11]Batchelor, G.K. (1967), An introduction to fluid dynamics, Cambridge UP
(reprinted 2000).

BOOK 2

LONGITUDINAL CELESTIA

Canto 7 – On earth
– for John Clarke

The question of direction along barrel
of world's unlikely toroidal motion
confounds business of usual exchanges
within given walls calculated
to minimize the risk sideways
glances introduce to Newton's dream

Who knows who's really beside you
at the dinner table is a question
easily answered only by those
without the sense to go out
in the rain where falling heavens
ante up damp paradaisal intimations

Push against your feet ratchets
up the stakes while further deliberations
anticipate unlikely guests and Walt's
sea in all its wavy insistence refusing
to be mere instance much less
reference calls into question wet

William Harvey, 1651, notes pulse
and substance form together,[12] first
life in stuff beating, but why not
beat stuffing, as if that whole
wave and particle thing[13] hadn't
happened or the mere memory of sublime

Tootie apparitions taking the top
off the works and dumping you

---

[12] "What central pulse – and you the heart," Walt Whitman, *Leaves of Grass.*
For a somewhat different perspective, see Jack Spicer's *Language*, "Thing
Language 1." See also fn 11 above.

[13] "The tidal swell / Particle and wave / Wave and particle / Distances." Lan-
guage, "Love Poems 5," Jack Spicer

head first out there with Pip[14]
contaminates instance's demand
for attention constricted to non-
resonating Yankee rock pile, whatever

sequel invention dances out
of its countless chambers to whirl
in a swirl of Ellingtonian swing
repercussions continue to register
across a wide swath of the floor
sweeping us off our feet into arms

of earth's non-harmonic vibratory dip
and up like the white knight in the looking
glass lifting off and returning with all
kinds of junk and occasional damp
intimations of wave's further
longitudinal irregularities beyond wet

---

[14] ". . . Pip's ringed horizon began to expand around him miserably." Herman
Melville, "The Castaway," *Moby-Dick.*

Canto 8 – Usual exchanges
– *for Ed Dorn*

Three years after George W. Bush Jr.
admitted to the world there were no
weapons of mass destruction thus
exposing the Great Lie he had used
to unleash uncontrollable blood letting
on a people who founded human
civilization more Americans than ever
just stated their belief the war was necessary
to eliminate said non-existent weapons

Is this a case of civilization's auto-cannibalistic
destiny, some final withering of the flower
rooted in Enkidu's seduction in a vast
settling into glazed eyes and inextendible
declensions of harmonic vistas all git up
in purple mountain's kick ass majesty
fluttering diaphanously around lady
liberty's surgically augmented charms
designed to excite maximum national
tumescence in really tight jeans?

The Battle Hymn of the Republic
was pretty hard, too, and Onward
Christian Soldiers caused more swelling
than your typical school board
was comfortable with though seven
year olds exposed to coming operations
in inflicted devotions and armed Jesus
penetrations within hallowed equestrian
intimations could already hear falling
towers symphonic ode to democratic

missionary position's inevitable viral
rendition of Bend Over, World
banging around in Sousa modulated
regulatory rhythms designed to synchronize
boogie apparitions and Tootie declensions
into simulated gravy *unum* arrangements
of formerly *pluribus* tainted wiggle
contamination's multiple pie orgies
and shameless adoration of erupting
hoots and jelly roll funk declarations.

Canto 9 – Falling heaven's ante
– for Richard Rathwell

Are you in or out is not just a question
Savonarola might have put to that
Sforza guy,[15] thus laying groundwork

for endless variations to proceed
until face to face with Bob
Dylan[16] or at least someone who seems

to sing like that in a sentence he had
never anticipated he removes
the stick from his posterior apparatus

and gets down. Getting down is connected
to rain just as in and out tends toward
unalloyed speculation on possible

position's relative razz factor and slippage
as more than an accident of broken
or misplaced traction. Ante suggests

the green shade over heaven's eyes
is not simply a sign, thus converting
sensible representations into footwear

appropriate for terrain widely considered
to violate consensual practices banned
in Texas where rain is not known

to go out much thus raising eyebrows
as to its preferences behind the famous
door where it has been said unspeakable

---

[15] "Under the baldachino, silver'd with heavy stitches / Bianca Visconti, with
   Sforza / The peasant's son and the duchess, / to Rimini, and to the wars
   southward. . .," Ezra Pound, "Canto VIII," *The Cantos.*
[16] "You don't need a weather man to know which way the wind blows," Bob
   Dylan, "Subterranean Homesick Blues," *Bringin' It All Back Home.*

damp intimations occasionally
cohabit in specific postures outlawed
in various Christian republics and less

sanitary public washrooms.[17] Bob says
God, you must be putting me on
and Savonarola searching the sky for signs

of rain while not concurring
seems to indicate he'd be happy to jump
ship of only he could get down

and out *sans* brolly to boogy till the cows
passed by in paradaisal accumulations
of released damp *domos* variations.

---

[17] "Sensible representation indicates of itself that its truth is 'in' as well as
'outside' it," Jean-Luc Nancy.

Canto 10 – Temporary Concilia

Whatever measure you bring to this
odd business of coming and going and
going and going it's never less than
that brush of wings against your cheek[18],
concilia, yes, sweet as late season peaches
just as briefly implicated in fortunate
reversals and untended patches
of extraordinary stones, each ablaze
with singular flame only they know
in their hard, bounded tongues emptied
of all spurious intimations of punctual
harbinger's artifice's dolled up
majesty and laurel load

Left to its own devices it begs the question
for more sustained suspensions, more
interrogatory essences distilled into flight's
fancy toroidal arabesques and distant
aberration's unlikely combination's refusal
to stoop to explanatory degradation
when pleasure of having met belly
up to the bar cannot be measured
in terms other than irrefragable
and evanescent quotidian dado possibilities
multiplied by unique combinatory
beauty mechanism's unlikely articulation
and stunned repetition formula's ever-shifting
arrangements of evaporating Razzamatootie.[19]

---

[18] "My, people come and go so quickly here" Dorothy Gale, *The Wizard of Oz.*

[19] "Because true works have done (as I often say) with the official canon, /
leapt into the line as it has always been: fluid / to be those where the divi-
sion of the line was independent." Victor Coleman, "G, Independently of a
Debate on Form," *MAL ARME, Letter Drop 3.*

Big bang instigations expanding pie
vectors spin katastematic pleasure[20]
functions past stabilizing foundation
dreams into restless assurances
of ordinary's expanding articulation
into Emersonian jelly roll funk
eruption's artesian voice intimation
that *plain old you and me.*[21] Smoke
and mirrors ain't the half of it if
you take into account Tootie calibrations
and post-quantum bop time wine dark
delta broiling with flows multiple
and magnificent, so that even stones
openly speak of variable distances.

---

[20] "If you wish to make Pythocles rich, do not increase his means, but dimish his desire," Epicurus. Quoted in *Lives of the Philosophers* by Diogenes Laertius.

[21] "We thrive by casualities. Our chief experiences have been casual," Ralph Waldo Emerson, "Expreience."

Canto 11 – Tenuous domains of unstable weather

The laughter of streaming water
is a language only available

during tenuous domain's unstable
weathers concoct in the night drifts

through our eyes bearing shadows
unlikely promise of alien intrusions

at the dinner table and unexpected
outcome's provocation within exceeded

bounds former notation of rescripted
hoots and hollers, church within

a church Zinzendorf called his damp
paradaisal intimations of modalities

of love and its feasts[22] extending
angular domestications past longitudinal

distortions inevitable declensions
of Razz into effusively executed

instances of fulsome prison human
blues till human already up

against the wall wheels about
belting out a raucous rendition

of Auld Lang Syne only to find
the screws vamoosed, the door

---

[22] "May thy first holy / wound anoint me for the conjugal / Business upon that member of / my Body, which is for the benefit / of my wife; and the Purple red oil / flow upon my Priest's Hole, and / make it rightly fitted for the / Procurator's Business," Count Nicholas Ludwig von Zinzendorf, "Hymn 2114," translated from the German by H.D.

wide open and all time spilling
out in a swirl of restless tempos

scatter across crumbling ground
hotly pursued by the Vanishing Point

and its posse of substantive interrogations
demanding to know who did it, who

might have done it and when it will be
O.K. to declare victory and get the hell

out of the range home once claimed
now crawling with irregular devices.

Canto 12 – Inextendible paths backwards

They're backward because forward
as a state seceded and regrouped
as some forsaken accumulation
of large wooden horses bearing
geeks gibbering blithely of soft
wet reception's flowers and chocolate
and large groups of desert dwelling
Kantians doing the Wave
across Arabia Felix[23]

What a moment that was, light
everywhere, your honey reasonable
as hell and all the world laid out
in squares at your feet, the path
to the stone shining numbers
cross your heart blues recalling
inevitable resolutions bearing distant
formulations of numerical relations
hot diggety vanishing dog

In any case if it's all a collusion
deluded of trees, then angle
of declension fouling innermost
lingering glimmer as it casts
about in tightening spaces
seeking remains of last stand
in images of Tootie formations
is commensurate to any stuttering
whirlwind they can conjure[24]

---

[23] "Freedom's untidy, and free people are free to make mistakes and commit crimes and do bad things. They're also free to live their lives and do wonderful things, and that's what's going to happen here," Donald Rumsfeld.

[24] "As if, on some other frequency, or out of the eye of some whirlwind rotating too slow for her heated skin even to feel the centrifugal coolness of, words were being spoken." Thomas Pynchon, *The Crying of Lot 49*.

The vanishing point meanwhile
having bit the big one exits
stage right half the furniture
in tow leaving not only certain
exposed intimations of damp
smelly heavens contesting with busted
up bits of former landscape replete
with bovine verisimilitude's ungulate
relation to scenery but baring

in process luminescent deceptions
stalking in the wings where free
floating unlinked copies do the soft
shoe off stage in orders leave
old ways looking vaguely
dazed among crumbling scenarios
invariably wretched memories of last
Sunday's frozen T.V. dinner increasingly
fraught over hapless foundling destinies

BOOK 3

ASTONISHING PARADES
OF NULLITY

"No one speaks English and everything is broken."
– Tom Waits

Canto 13 – Time

Each time is the time and no reach
can reach beyond walls decreed out
of declensions of Razzamatootie warp

its woof. Now Guelph now Ghibilene now
chicken pies till the cows come home now
nothing but Africa's agony sold

into servitude no pie can surmount. Poor
Dante, trudging those gorgeous hills
the poem unwinding through shattered

laminar dreams of home and parades
of nullity testifies luck of the draw
is no patsy you can bull around

like some Tootie in a bad movie
about unforeseen collisions of collateral
passion leading inevitably to whatever

end dictates pieces' facile arrangements
in baggy justice ignores cracked stones
hieroglyphic telegraphy regarding

ice's attitude in certain circumstances
toward whatever gets in its way. Living
in its shadow did the fools have a harder

time breeding wars out of dead brains
fantasy of mass destruction's inevitable
materialization in instruments of razzle

dazzle degrades Razz into one more
disposable instance of insatiable blank
gaze sustained by moral rectumtude's

laminar formations of well-armed
stupidities? It slaps against rocks now
still smelling of ice, speaking of old

tongues' lugubrious interventions
in ethereal buzz nourishes stars
with lapping laughter rolls in

unreckoned in nets of advanced
rigmarole bedecked with whatever
garlands currently are on sale[25]

---

[25] "The arts have been consumed by society in the same way the masses have,"
Sylvère Lotringer.

Canto 14 – Declensions of razzamatootie

Should have known the deviation
would enter as soon as moment's walls
breached through obscure back door given
Dolphesque clamour contaminating best
laid attempts to reform Razz's Tootie calibrations
into spread sheets when unexpected corners
requiring star nourishment merely to hold
out against recurring laminar fantasies
resembling crowds of cows on their way home.[26]

Deviating cows largely occur at
inopportune moments, moments whose walls
have suffered irreparable structural
contamination leaving them gasping for a return
to good, honest derazzified erections
contained within generation's non-ethereal
hump necessities blessed by reference
to tracks inalienable discretion along
line of least insistent bovine infatuation
until even home itself arrests no fine tooth cows.[27]

Expansion as general modus operandi
resonates at extreme frequencies even
Buzz Corey[28] often interpreted as alien
along the lines of Philip K. Dick's pink
beam[29] and ensuing cellular nova states'
alteration of both the void and the thing's
ever receding dance's Epicurean wiggle

---

[26] "Whence does the aether nourish the stars?" Lucretius, *De Rerum Natura*
[27] "The normal / kind are not abnormal, not / different than the cows when they're / friendly . . .," Canto 37.
[28] See *Space Patrol,* episode 129, "The Man Who Stole a City," June 13, 1953.
[29] "A flash of pink light blinded me. 'Oh my god,' I said." "VALIS, as living information, would penetrate the world, replicating in human brains, cross-bonding with them and assisting them, guiding them, at a subliminal level, which is to say, invisibly." Philip K. Dick, *Valis.*

factor incursions as they spin nebular
arms out to embrace dark matter's
unaccountable proclivity toward grace.

Such pleasures as Tuscan hills offer
their towers rising amid clouds of swallows
punctuate Dante's stern voice as it soars
polyphonically accompanying dreams
of damnation and tender young promise
of roseate salvation's damp paradaisal
fig intimations but all dolled up
in white and various belts of pure
non-deviating cincture vectors leaves
heaven ensnared in dehydrating enclosures.

Canto 15 – Moment's walls

Falling towers mark evaporating
image seeds and whole worlds drifting
into the rafters to dissipate among
dreams cut loose from any sense
of common destiny and binding
intimations of wine dark exteriorities
against swelling sea Walt wrote
out of and equal to in diversion's
corrosive sublimation of further pulse

What sneaks in wrests incalculable distance
from bounded forebodings of Yankee rock
pile walls criss-crossing demonic
vistas with non-resonating matrix
incursions. Also known as *Henry's
nick*,[30] it doles out dolor along with steaming
pies as if hoot inflections simply marked
ever shifting edges of incommensurable
celestial middle passage's non-stop

devouring promise's end of any human
sheen, that last lingering insistence
on Vanishing Point's claim to reach
some edge within which massive exports
of freedom and democracy fall like pennies
over parched lands and inverted brolly
injunctions[31] ring from shining shore
to promised lands' insouciant hope
antidote while outside with all that

---

[30] ". . . I have been anxious to improve the nick of time, and notch it in my
    stick, too; to stand on the meeting of two eternities . . . to toe that line,"
    Henry David Thoreau.
[31] "Just make sure that your umbrella is upside down." "Pennies from Heaven,"
    Johnnie Burke and Arthur Johnston.

teeming and unsanitary anti-regulatory
infection dances madcap red masque hoedowns
to demonic Bob Wills fiddles. Wanting
for nothing leaves inert dreams enthroned
and confounds hell's clamour at gate
of further indications, dampening
hoot burst's temporal expansion
involuntary ejaculatory response
screeches with harmonic mechanisms

polyunsaturated equalities and intentional
gestures of goodwill so that moment's
walls then rise square and straight
as a Moose Jaw optometrist leaving
unsecured angular aberrations adrift
and subject to moral rectumtudes
outraged accusations of preternatural
posturing's wanton metaphysical
sodomite violations of temporal purity.

Canto 16 – Shattered laminar dreams
– *for Victor Coleman*

All because you can't keep your fingers
off the damn thing[32], twiddling when you
ought to be focused on getting
balanced columnar irrelevancies aligned
with neo-traditional harmonic preservations
of past participle's dehydrated Tootie principle.[33]

Descending into unrequited dreams
of democratic vistas I turns and watches
itself turn into recollected bits
and pieces, that old gathering all dolled up
in frilly declensions of frock logic
implying substantial accumulations

of unlikely *veritas* mirages shimmering
across highway might amount to more
than proverbial hills' consequent emission's
banal exhalations and odd lexical
conglomerates. So much for lyrical
braces and wine dark celestial

contractions resembling climactic stellar
spunk gushes which up and walk
out in a tiff of offended poetic
sensibilities trailing clouds of metonymy
and metaphorical solemnity behind
firmly held instruments of polite

---

[32] Cf, fn 3.
[33] "Transition equals tradition," Craig Harris, "Bluocracy," *Political Blues*.

well-groomed discourse.[34] Stable exclamations
of approval whine that vatic violations
of agreed upon silence's dampening *unum*
compulsions demanding civil and sober
Ken and Barbie gallery *politesse* as a pre-requisite
for disposition of art booty

to duly sponsored dissident calculation
and efficiency zombies elevates intoxication
beyond acceptable hygienic norms as determined
in units of degrees Calvin. Absolute zero
in this frame radiates through sobriety
guaranteeing mediocre ascensions

and countless reassuring pats on the back
asserting that disturbances of unrestrained
and frankly rude incursions of sibylline static[35]
along the line of least recurrent lexical implosions
and neutron star-like articulations of immediate
chthonic densities will be expelled immediately.

---

[34] "We may therefore formulate as follows: the ghost of some simple metre
should lurk behind the arras in even the 'freest' verse; to advance menacingly
as we doze, and withdraw as we rouse. Or, freedom is only truly freedom
when it appears against the background of an artificial limitation." T.S.
Eliot, "Reflections on 'Vers Libre'." See also Canto 1, "Chicken Pie."

[35] "The Sibyl of Cumae protected the Roman Republic and gave timely
warnings. In the first century C.E. she foresaw the murders of the Kennedy
brothers, Dr. King and Bishop Pike. She saw the two common denomina-
tors of the four murdered men: first, they stood in defense of the liberties
of the Republic; and second, each man was a religious leader. For this they
were killed. The Republic had once again become an empire with a ceasar.
'The Empire never ended.'" Philip K. Dick, *Tractates: Cryptica Scriptura,* 15.

Canto 17 – Collisions of collateral passion

The lost worlds of Ellington bang
and knock against young grumbling
reluctant to move beyond disposable
regimes of discounted anger repackaged

in razzle dazzle corruptions of simulated
gravy's unconscionable dreams of doggy
hotels replete with heated pools, feather
beds and five star meals. Whole worlds

fade and stumble and music that cleared
the sky for further incursions of time
formations seeding tomorrow with razzified
Tootie precipitations is relegated to the back

of forgotten drawers along with the Paris
Commune and 1968. Unpremeditated acts
of lascivious mediation elevate otherwise
deferred buzzing *porne* constitutions

to unsettled proclamations of emancipatory
Walden apparitions etched in evaporating
moments' residual streams of tears
and exclamations of damp, cellular contractions

the pulse situated in molecular reformation
extracting itself in resonant imbroglios. Razz
rises among the ashes howling for Tootie to join
him in bang's lingering vibratory sub-woofer

wiggle instigation, the sub-voce of dark
matter's night song, its inter-stellar hoochy
koochy croon and together they burn
across indigo skies making no claim on further

swaths, lighting the aether with veils of flickering
vanishing acts and pointless pirouettes etching
unpremeditated figures of confusing and sometime
boring anti-*veritas* incursions.[36] Meanwhile back

beckons as always, not toward erotic
combustions as they configured antic mind songs[37]
among bedraggled intimations of further
worlds in ordinary time, but as intensity's

demand for original and unique statements
of navel's singularly specular claim to precious
formulations designed to satisfy editorial demands
for pre-established anti-thinking satisfactions[38].

---

[36] "Boredom is part of the Logos, too." Jack Spicer.
[37] Cf. Robin Blaser, *The Moth Poem*.
[38] "Dear Mike, I have never needed to understand works of art. I don't like or
revel in something because I understand it," Anonymous editor.

Canto 18 – Weapons of mass razzle dazzle

Further unraveling notations to the contrary
opens a final movement of temporary
concilia extracted *contra natura* and with
living memory's sad arrangement of once again
down the garden path of unnoticed
coercions and inflicted devotions all dolled
up in erectile excitement's tales of current fashion

Exporting democracy in this sense amounts
to proverbial hills' consequent exhalations
augmented with rhetorical simplifications
unerring garble factor frequently adorned
with floral imagery and intense metaphorical
turns down picturesque lanes crowded
with cows. Coming as no surprise

coagulating meaning interrupts attempts
at diverting seamless instances vanishing
resistance, swelling with untoward
admonitions regarding market based
truth disseminations and general gas
emissions strapped into pilot suits
and parachutes buckled up to maximize

bulging crotch testimonials to presidential
manhood's assurance erectile certitude's
control systems are go. The contribution
of rolled socks to visual signals heavy
breathing invocations and massive
unipolar instrumentalities cannot
be detailed due to stabilized embargos

of *veritas* incursions and vino revelations
also known as consensus expulsion's
daily reality pie served up steaming
and ready for instant consumption

with your venti de-caf non-fat
latte. The unavoidable *passing away* of tens
of thousands of Iraqis while in pursuit

of democratic vistas ineluctable
calculations of packaged benefits
accruing to deal's apotheosis in unlimited
deposits of material substantive's market
values should be understood strictly
in terms of pagan exchange's weight
function in the glimmering scales of capital.

BOOK 4

MORAL RECTUMTUDES

"If I knew for certain that a man was coming to my home with the conscious design of doing me good, I should run for my life."
– Henry David Thoreau, *Walden*.

Canto 19 – Banal exhalations

What smells is not so much the carcass
too long in last light's dwindling

thermal emissions as leaking remnants
of last year's guaranteed certitude

regarding fallacious combinatory
agent's power to transubstantiate

proverbial hills' *porne* emissions
into consecrated exhalations of meat free

orders of non-messy, moistureless
luv zombies.[39] The incidence of reflection

declines proportionately to the magnitude
of density of simulated angelic

stabilizer mass. Then doing good looks
like a cement truck, but all cleaned up

and decorated with transcendent
meditative reflections of quick set

dreams harbouring secrets of Jimmy
Hoffa's ultimate proclivity towards unrequited

vanishing points' inestimable determination
of frequently forgotten foundational

inclusions on which erections of grand
filigreed splendor rest sure in evasions

---

[39] "The Atonists got rid of their spirit 1000s of years ago with Him. The flesh
is next. Plastic will soon prevail over flesh and bones. Why is it Death you
like? Because then no 1 will keep you up all night with that racket dancing
and singing." Ishmael Reed, *Mumbo Jumbo.*

of interrogatory penetrations might
otherwise reveal deeply contaminated

confusions and boring absence
of intensities bind bones and other

materials quietly vibrating to messages
reeking of Sirian business in stable

formations suitable for large scale exterior
extensions and vibratory excitement

suppression architecture's spatial
resemblance to big box store injunctions

to forget any awkward claims of reason
beyond lower taxes' sacred compulsion status.

Canto 20 – Just say no

After having said it does the contraction
protect essential pre-existing lack

of circulation from the threat expansion
or hidden signals in dark matter's

background radiation[40] designed to seduce
even the most wary and unspoiled

into degrading and compromising positions
pose to anti-hoot arrangements and ongoing

suppression of erupting gravy celebrations
and pie in the face mitochondrial destiny

determinations? On the other hand
offers at least a refraction of broken

but persistent inclinations leading
down and possibly out of badly wallpapered

containment strategies all dolled up
as collective agreement on homeward's

inevitable prize for bold poetic
expression. Unauthorized abandonment

of powerful metaphoric necessities
result in automatic benching

and compulsory excision from lists
of approved teaching tools, thus elevating

---

[40] "The composition of dark matter is unknown, but may include new elementary particles such as WIMPs, axions, and ordinary and heavy neutrinos, as well as astronomical bodies such as dwarf stars, planets collectively called MACHOs and clouds of nonluminous gas." Wikipedia.

Urizenic two step inhibitory exclusion
compulsions which eloquently declaim

rational critical principles' defense
of bovine intentions even as they fade

into knowing *what they like*[41] along with
Vanishing Point's undeclared but violent claim

on corners, shadows, and spatial torsions
twist Tootie's arm up and back until all

multiversal emissions and universal boundary
leakages are recontained within eternal Uncle.

---

[41] Often identified with mysterious incursions of inviolable truth waves ema-
nating from the pineal gland.

Canto 21 – The war on everything bad

The *unum* reflex mode eliminating
pockets of resistance and promising as many

chickens as your little pot can hold
and supersized helpings of genuine simulated

gravy and biscuits stipulates various lexical
formations identified as undermining

martial determination's bulging crotch
regulatory compulsions will be bound

blindfolded to predetermined sticks
in the mud and subjected to multiple

indignities including arbitrary assertions
of sleeper cell infections wired up to direct

pre-frontal insertions of lyrical intensities
draped in morose or alternately ecstatic

you fill in the blank declensions of I
metaphorically amplified to resemble

the Vanishing Point dressed in trench
coat and more than happy to reveal

well-hung inclinations toward self
exposure as a matter of unquestionable

faith in the inevitable conquest of spatial
aberrations as part of the overall program

of landscaping the way down to look
like a Wal-Mart parking lot. Heavily armed

cows provide more than adequate
security and are perfectly willing to assist

the rerouting of unauthorized violations
of intense word configurations back into first

knee jerk disposition toward what they know
they like, a kind of ungulate cud insistence

on eliminating eruptions of razzed out
lexical deformations known to be inimical

to image formations bearing assurances
the war on everything bad starts here

Canto 22 – Hanging Saddam

The marriage of justice and payback in popular
determinations of repeated rolling heads

garners huge ratings and deep satisfactions
regarding successful prosecution of vague

wars guaranteed to achieve protected
shopping environments except occasionally

in Salt Lake City. Random acts of terror
can be differentiated from large groups

of cows on their way home by the way
the dangle proceeds and whether or not the head

detaches due to gravity's weakened
but never the less sufficient force

as it traverses adjacent multiverses[42]
inundating local key lime cheesecake

with just enough juice to keep it
steady. This is not a case of Lady

Day's strange fruit since that lacks
entrepreneurial deregulated bonding formations

in defense of *unum* regulations and *pale* –
not as it marks off barbarous incursions

from imperial century projects but as a sign
of a dream of undiluted Lawrence Welk

---

[42] "Lee Smolin has suggested that every black hole is the seed for a new
universe that erupts into existence through a big bang-like explosion, but
is forever hidden from our view by the black hole's event horizon." Brian
Greene, *The Elegant Universe*.

variations permeating the aether and leaking
from star to star. Similarities, however,

include pendulous consequences[43]
beyond undulating afterthoughts

as they burst into the street in flows
of incommensurable righteousness claims

while visions of Viva el Muerte,[44] a dark
dude last seen haunting the site

of poetry's bloody demise, trip delicately
around hilltop oracular expulsions.[45]

---

[43] "The sweep of the pendulum had increased in extent by nearly a yard. As
a natural consequence its velocity was also much greater. But what mainly
disturbed me was the idea that it had perceptibly *descended.*" Edgar Allen
Poe, "The Pit and the Pendulum."
[44] October 12, 1936.
[45] "So that after much time and many arguments had been spent to bring
[Mrs. Hutchinson] to see her sin, but all in vain, the church with one con-
sent cast her out." John Winthrop, Journals, March 22, 1638.

Canto 23 – Inordinate concupiscence

The number of times per week varies
according to availability of post-quantum
indwelling chronos circulations.[46] Half

past one struggles for release into deciduous
adumbrations of unspeakable proclivities
toward temporal profusion's post-meridian

quickies. But it don't mean a thing if
machinic synchronization brings
agreement to sway majestically

detached from whim's vulgar propensity
to breed in dark corners.[47] There's no
accounting for the taste of seminal

extrusions as they emit morphogenetic
vibratory seduction waves, promising
non-obligatory nooners as a pardaisal

option to papal visions of pre-Cartesian
hunky-dory. Fleeing numbers note
breached boundaries have increased

desperate retrenchments of ordinal
derazzification rendering laminar
equilibration thick and chunky to eyes

---

[46] "Homeorrhetic means at least that the rhesis flows, but similarity pushes upstream and resists. All the temporal vectors possessed in a directional arrow are here, in this place, arranged in the shape of a star. What is an organism? A sheaf of times. What is a living system? A bouquet of times." Michael Serres, "The Origin of Language."

[47] "Creative chaos is illegality itself, for its description dissolves the distinction between the macroscopic state and the microscopic fluctuation; correlations can appear among distant events; local deviations echo throughout the system – the matrix state in which the fluctuations are amplified and from which things are born." Ilya Prigogine and Isabel Stengers, "Dynamics from Leibniz to Lucretius."

hungry for scalar ascension's salacious
hankering after tidy outcomes
of a profitable nature.[48] Skulking

past interminable clarities of duplicitous
insertions leaves untold anxious
diversions counting on willful blindness

as an oracular correspondence to belted
purities of singular affirmations. Countless
damp, hot provocations to the contrary

indicate stiffening approaches to numinous
openings of a delicate nature may succeed
in asyntactical violations[49] celestial lockdown

counts among hardest cases of wild
intimations' assault on self-contained
instances non-reflective happily-ever-afters.

---

[48] "A penny saved is a penny earned." Benjamin Franklin, "Poor Richard's
Almanac."

[49] "Dozens of slightly dampened fashionable candle holders made of yellow
saffron / Their reflections harsh against this foolproof and indispensable
bathroom shelf, / prior to the satisfaction provided by a box of chocolates? .
. ." Victor Coleman, Mal Atme, "U – A Sheet of Beaten Gold."

Canto 24 – Wobbling Columbian recession

The agony of an untoward estimation
seems overwrought in the light of further

defenestration undertakings. The Columbians
have receded and this fact establishes

beyond itself suggestions of secession's
pellicular threat emissions as means

of instant mass emulsification into renditions
of hallelujah chorus rewritten in colour

coded assurances everything will soon be under
the gun will continue abated by regular

announcements to the contrary. Deciduous
alarms signaling all clear conundrums

leave bend-and-kiss protocols to fend for
certain trains of thought[50] while maintaining

awkward postures grievous defense against
darker, hirsute bearers of unwelcome

signifiers from shady pasts and parts unknown
to the Project Managers. Aberrant frequency

variations then invade the viral stabilizer and all hell
breaks into antiphonal choruses[51] till wobbling

---

[50] "The assurance of thought is inseparable from its restlessness – and its restlessness, as drunkenness, is at once an anxiety and an exhalation, the risk and the transport of relation." Jean Luc Nancy, *Hegel: the Restlessness of the Negative.*

[51] Cf.. Carla Bley, Steve Swallow and Andy Shepherd, "Wrong Key Donkey."

differentials collapse returning monophonic
rectitude to threatened proliferations of unregulated

captivation. The damage having been
introduced to its own devices recalls

poultry paeans and hoot eruptions from dim
recesses of Razzamatootie continues to buzz

under the radar of archonic inhibitory
advisories.[52] But broad strokes leave them

reconfigured in extreme extenuations resembling
uninvited guests lined up to cart off the gardening

and dishwashing work while leaving
the Vanishing Point hog tied and sodomized.[53]

---

[52] "One day, Shuzanghu said to his wife, 'How long must we live without a place to rest our feet?'" Dhammai legend.

[53] "Have you noticed more and more people speaking different languages at the supermarket? Schools? Movies? At your local bank? Have you noticed radio stations and TV crackling with Spanish or other languages in our English speaking America?" Frosty Wooldridge, culture expert.

BOOK 5

INSANITARY
BACKYARD ABSTRACTIONS

Canto 25 – With liberty and justice for all

The descent's gradual revelation occurs
not in topographical inclinations

leading predictably to pits and scatological
revelry rendered in armed image

excursions through typically pornophobic
relish.[54] Verbal litter marks the way

crumpled words sticky with a sheen
of distantly remembered gravy long

gone to sedimentary encrustations
and the rise of discursive zombie apparati

resembling Mel Gibson three sheets
to the wind and holding righteously

forth on theological subtleties of liberty's
glorious guarantee of sugar tit floozy

regulatory temptation opportunities.[55]
Who winds up there anticipates

heavily armoured engineering assaults
on pools of words drained and reclaimed

for development by veritas platforms
and unum foundations seeking coherence

---

[54] "There is a hell, i.e. all those who die in personal mortal sin, as enemies of God, and unworthy of eternal life, will be severely punished by God after death. On the nature of mortal sin, see SIN; on the immediate beginning of punishment after death, see PARTICULAR JUDGMENT. As to the fate of those who die free from personal mortal sin, but in original sin, see LIMBO (*limbus parvulorum*)." Catholic Encyclopedia.

[55] "Man is thus metamorphosed into a thing, into many things." Ralph Waldo Emerson, "The American Scholar."

amid the spent and steaming lexical heaps
deposited consequent to arguing declarations

of bovine independence and constitutional
demands for tax relief. It does get

darker,[56] though no rational cow
would ever confuse that with objective

correlatives or metaphorical confusions
of vehicular ontology. Home, after all,

is where the heart is served up stewed with local
root veggies according to neo-traditional

recipes approved by health officials and listed
as nutritious and safe for mass consumption.[57]

---

[56] "Soit / que / l'Abime / blanchi / étale / furieux / sous une inclinaison / plane
désespérément / d'aile / le sienne / par / avance retombée d'un mal à dresser
le vol / et couvrant les jaillissements / coupant au ras les bonds / trés à l'inté-
rieur résume / l'ombre enfouie dans le profodeur par cette voile alternative .
. .." Stéphane Mallarmé, *Un Coup de Des.*

[57] "If you like you can sit out / in the blue fumes. You can / have a whole oat
bran wheat / muffin and an immaculate water." Gilbert Sorrentino, "Old
Palo Alto Classic."

Canto 26 – Freedom fries

The grease no doubt remains the same, thick
with the stench of saturated rhetoric
and two or three centuries worth of armed
eliminations dressed up in a three
thousand dollar suit and looking good
enough to instigate endless debates
in which both sides agree to implement
binding parades of nullities on all parties
preceding universal declarations of victory.[58]

Life, liberty and the pursuit of happiness show up
disguised as Larry, Curly, and Moe doing
passable imitations of Dubya, Dick and Condi
dolled up as the four horsemen of the apocalypse
minus one. Subsequent developments
lead to lewd brouhahas in which scarlet
pimps[59] demand legislative transmogrifications
of spit swapping into liberty kisses and a certain
sexually transmitted unspeakableness

into the democracy disease.[60] Not to be out
done in Gallic exclusionary purification
extractions, large parties of spontaneously
armed men with beards and baseball caps
reluctantly leave big sky country aiming
to pull down that freedom whore[61]
eastern bastards have set up in New York

---

[58] "Cold comes creeping in the window / And in the sky searchlights sweep / countryside / O frozen lonliness that will not thaw / Nor let me sleep." John Wieners, "The Serpent Hiss."

[59] "They seek him here, they seek him there, those Frenchies seek him every-where." Sir Percy Blakeney.

[60] See Hieronymus Fracastorius (Girolamo Fracastoro), "Syphilis sive morbus gallicus" (1530).

[61] "We will not forget that Liberty has here made her home; nor shall her chosen altar be neglected." Grover Cleveland.

harbour like some giant hollow horse
and send the bitch back where she

came from, or better yet load her up
in a B-52 and drop her on the camel
jockeys. In quick succession beans, bread,
cuffs, salad dressing, horns, and toast
are rounded up in a dragnet and marched
blindfolded into the U.S. Congress
where they are piled on top of each other
in a pyramidal lexicon of Gaulish

derived linguistic sleeper cell intent
stripped naked and subjected to various
cavity searches while the pursuit of happiness
looks on in august and judicious disinterest
till Moe pops him upside the head and War
ever the joker, instigates a vast and proliferating
entanglement emanating beyond bulging
crotch solutions' leave the whole apparatus
dangling limply while freedom fries.

Canto 27 – Democratic vistas

Somewhere near the bottom in spite
of de Crevecoeur's mediated farmer's
spotless Sunday buckboard theological
declarations of dissipated castle formations,
polyunsaturated fats render whatever
Ellingtonian dreams arose from street's
impeccable beat into harbingers of clogged
but inexpensive cornucopia delusions
mounted on truck frames and guaranteed
to wipe out anything gets in their way.[62]

Hell's hand basket is paved with bovine
intentions aligned in egalitarian lattice
structures.[63] The way home then looks
both ways before crossing but often
misses erratic diversions and random
violations of anticipatory conclusion
jumping which bears down on pedestrian
declarations and constitutional delusions
with all the fury of unleashed
intimations of recalcitrant elitist laughter.

Finding your way through all that tenacious
closure and endless resolution
while attending to perennial Clanton's
lurking in the bush or outside
the window[64] declaiming virtues
of unrestricted access while looking down
barrels aimed at your back in the name
of equality's guaranteed dream of hand
in hand down primrose lane toward shining

---

[62] "They adopt democratic manners. They foam at the mouth. They hate."
Ralph Waldo Emerson, "Experience."
[63] "He had a dream and it shot him." Huckleberry Finn.
[64] The rifle shots entered the lighted billiard parlor through a glass-windowed
locked door which opened from the rear of the parlor onto a dark alley,
which ran between Allen and Fremont Streets, along the side of the parlor.

futures often leaves you at a loss
for alternatives to wild-eyed declarations
of infernal eruptions. Meanwhile some *enfant*
sauvage dances in the gutter grinning
sadly and pointing a blue stained finger
at a large concatenation of cows fending
off errant instabilities and Tootie outbursts
with rousing choruses of home on the range
while resolutely insisting further operations'
elimination functions are good to go.

Canto 28 – The Right to Closure

When it entered the list of human
rights,[65] Razz was tempted to revert
to atavistic behaviours, having been bathed

in caustic imperatives and the prose
of Gilbert Sorrentino, no quarter
given as they said at the Alamo,

and none accepted, it seemed strange
given all the dead, the incommensurable
pain of those with indelible memories

of small dark rooms and strategically
applied currents, and the sheer magnitude
of unrestrained violence unleashed to return

discipline and neatness to world tottering
on the frightening verge of unstable
circulations of chaotic generosity and rogue

waves of selfless caring that closure
could seem anything other than a brutal
illusion of determined deflections designed

to nurture ongoing hallucinations
of apocalyptic heaven fixes and intimations
of immortality's unlikely con.[66] The Sense

of an Ending stands up and cheers
for the home team as they straggle
by in ungulate bliss, udders adrift

---

[65] We have been denied closure." Anonymous Chilean on the death of the
mass murderer, Pinochet.
[66] "If someone says, 'I have a body' he can be asked, 'Who is speaking here
with this mouth?'" Ludwig Wittgenstein, *On Certainty*

in milky intimations of barnyard
manipular relief mechanisms and oneric
pancake formations, mistaking serial

hoof reflexes for ontological trajectories
and yet another declaration of victory
snatched from defeat's recurrent, puzzling

eruption into lingering dreams of Israelite
protection racket insinuations of recycled
glory and rivers of unrighteous blood[67]

spilled in name of paternal formations'
insistent demand for final elimination
of resistant unresolved sub-dominant chords.

---

[67] "Now, therefore, kill every male among the little ones, and kill every woman
who has known man by lying with him. But all the young girls who have not
known man by lying with him, keep alive for yourselves." Moses, *Numbers* 31:
17-19

Canto 29 – The defining conflict of our time

Chronologic assumptions of possessive
facticity punctuate conflicts laying claim
to insurmountable stabilities of in the first
place[68] as a vegetative contraction known
to take a figurative chain saw to actual

axis mundi leaving oozing amputated
stump to hobble to court on time
to lay charges.[69] The charges accumulate
rapidly reordering bipolar extenuations
into a sudden oracular point carves

out narrowing path into the mouth
of an hospitable interpretation function.
The way out limps,[70] staggers, stutters
singing past that, relocating the point
in choral arrangements leave it

sprouting up all over the place in stumped
interrogatives.[71] What defines the conflict
then insists that our time is not the place
we think it as while the conflict itself
contests any further implications rendering

infernal assessments of current events
beyond nightly reportage into desperate
terminations. No recognizable

---

[68] "'Tis only a question of time." R. W. Emerson, "Fate."
[69] "We shall have to face up squarely to the problem of why what one calls *historicism* is the result of the composition or of the explosion of the Hegalian system. We shall ask ourselves what is the *place* of history? Where is it enacted? Henry Corbin, "The Concept of Comparative Philosophy."
[70] "Some dissenters disagree womewhat / Other dissenters object / Rather more than not / But the great chiliastic heretic, Shoko Asahara ? Disagrees a lot." Edward Dorn, "Shoko."
[71] "What Champollion will decipher this hieroglyphic for us, that we may turn over a new leaf at last?" Henry David Thoreau, *Walden.*

adumbrations ameliorate predictable
protests limiting definitions to pellicular

amputations. Meanwhile Tootie
stirs the dark toward prepositional
ascensions designed to increase blood
flow engorging the night, hoping
some further interstitial encounter

might alter oracular confirmations
of faulty definitions.[72] But Our Time getting
hincky insists it has never been complicit
in unregulated penetrations of damp
quiddities and quickly slams the door shut.

---

[72] "America stands for liberty, for the pursuit of happiness, and for the unalien-
alienable right of life." George W. Bush, Washington, D.C., Nov. 3, 2003.

Canto 30 – Oracular confirmations

Sudden scheduled eruptions of *veritas*
confirmations emerge regularly in exchange
of orange blossom's smudge pot deal.[73]

Wild affirmations have been known to contradict
it against the better judgment of sundry
Managers, but no amount of equivocation

leads irresistibly to unforeseen crises
of intense foundational acquiescence. When
the bottom falls out, finding another

requirement for eruptive origins resists
quotidian serial aversions that might lead
otherwise past its conflicts into assertions

of unlikely lubricious couplings'
smoke hole implications[74] and unexpected
temporal variances leading beyond

into arrangements recognizable
for their partiality to provisional
insertions.[75] Oral interaction lays

claim to escaping jail shame
erects in the wake of cows on their way
home but unconfirmed reports of alien

---

[73] "You'd blow your nose, and it would be black," said Edward Camarena.

[74] "I take this evanescence and lubricity of all objects, which lets them slip through our fingers then when we clutch hardest, to be the most unhandsome part of our condition." Ralph Waldo Emerson, "Experience."

[75] "The terminal engagement portion prevents a connecting terminal which is provisionally inserted into the terminal housing chamber of the connector housing when the retainer is provisionally positioned with respect to the connector housing, from slipping off from the terminal housing chamber." United States Patent 6450841.

exigencies billowing in the draft
of excess expectations to the contrary
tend to evaporate in the absence

of textual materialization lost in typically
sulfurous thermal emissions of oracular
flatus associated with homeland

security. The Vanishing Point then enters
accompanied by fanfare and incense
blessing those gathered to celebrate

the immaculate knowledge of nothing
further all the while issuing
assurances regarding the integrity

of the levees as outlined in various reports
to the Project Managers who eagerly
declare victory before turning out the lights.

BOOK 6

ASCENDANT RHETORICAL SIMPLIFICATIONS

Canto 31 – The cows almost come home

Funny how the cows got in[76] and wouldn't
stop whatever insistent blundering
coagulated ungulate ganglia might seem
to propose in non-resistant telic dreams

Like everything else, it boggles various
unsettled accumulations of dear or
familiar trauma encrusted with
sedimentary determinations of self

congratulatory art tumescence.[77] Hardness
is a sign of home just as cows
can be counted on to mount
further endeavours in interest calculated

in compounded goal lines. It confounds
the ordinary, leaving it bleeding
in some filthy alley where cows usually
can't be bothered to slow down

having once again caught scent of accumulated
posterior emissions marking home's
dedicated inclination toward familiar
and dear formations of hollow horses

aligned in neo-Aquinian salvation
promissory instigations[78] to embrace

---

[76] "The cows cross at their own risk / declaring autonomous intentions . . .".
Canto 37

[77] ". . . the desert would meet us with a steady gale, dust, gray thorn bushes,
and hideous bits of tissue paper mimicking pale flowers among the prickles
of wind-tortured withered stalks all along the highway; in the middle of
which there sometimes stood simple cows, immobilized in a position (tail
left, white eyelashes right) cutting across all human rules of traffic." Vladimir
Nabokov, *Lolita*.

[78] "Then, too, in everlasting life is the full and perfect satisfying of every desire;
for there every blessed soul will have to overflowing what he hoped for and
desired." Thomas Aquinas.

non-promiscuous relational faith
certainties in face of unpredictable

pulsations arising somewhere on
the other hand and rolling ashore
in lugubrious intimations of unnamable
stellar contractions seminal infestation

of dark matter's mysterious wave
function giving rise to yet another
long shriek of alien enthusiasm denoting
further incursions of *oh yeah* and obscene

variations of modal instabilities' repeated
insensitivities to demands for textual
intensities designed to close the barn door
with feeling and minimal discursive digressions.

Canto 32 – Homeland Security

What they lock you up for doesn't know
how it's done, that casual agreement
along lines of least insistent intimation's
paradaisal wresting away of some
hammered thing into arrangements
of large wooden horses bereft of modal
variance's and finitude's wet lips.

Then there's the lingering question of *clasm*'s
derivation among emergent properties
and territorial claims surreptitiously indicated
in control driven anti-razzification
procedures designed to turn icons into elected
levee formations cows can comfortably
graze behind when the going gets tough

and the tough get refocused on pellicular
variations of shading as a matter not
so much of intelligence as necro-modal
cartological certainty formations[79]
all dolled up in sleeper-cell intimations
of alien intent to blow up fields
of dreams, convert the converted and remove

all Christmas trees from department
stores and malls thus leaving shopping
utterly bereft of divine consequences
and legally binding hope claims. Blanket
declarations assuring colour coded
determinations of unsurpassable peace
estimations echo in vast well-lit

---

[79] "'It is certain that we didn't arrive on this planet from another one hundred
years ago.' Well, it's as certain as such things *are*." Ludwig Wittgenstein, *On
Certainty*.

homilies to reasoned harmonies and dancing
images pre-approved for distribution
in democratically determined election
booth's reorganization of titular reigning
nominal claim to spatial stacking along lines
of least resistant expression quotient.[80]
Ensuing states of security appear in white

robes[81] intoning four-part harmonic paeans
to last year's garden as it rises in oneric
mists claiming singular status as non-reflective
image while jumping the queue everyone
thought indicated orderly evacuation procedures
before bend-and-kiss protocols kick in.[82]

---

[80] "Cold comes creeping in the window / And in the sky searchlights sweep
     / countryside / O frozen loneliness that will not thaw / Nor let me sleep."
     John Wieners, "The Serpent Hiss."
[81] cf. *Oh Brother, Where Art Thou?*
[82] "Help is on the way." David Murray, "Political Blues."

Canto 33 – Building a hopeful world

Well, there is a certain poignant almost
wistful where wist spreads out like fog
at Gilmore, California[83] and the cows
almost home give a huge sigh of relief
tone to it though the question of hope
tends to smell after a few days in the sun,
especially where thinning ozone,
greenhouse instigations, and bluster
exhalations contribute to gaseous
buildups known to be harmful to jelly roll
intimations and hopeless wiggle impulsions

Any further implications are persona
non grata among clusters of hopeful
converts issuing proclamations of individual
emancipatory reason gushes and declarations
of independently established pursuits
of universal right to closure as it
bypasses Odyssean stations in a fog
of bovine emissions blur the signage
warning of abandonment amid wild
tracks of formerly haunted approaches

to unsecured time.[84] Flattened and smoothed
in mills of constant interpretation
bordering on hostile states of exception
hope emerges large and sweet, quietly
queued up, inked finger raised in gesture
no doubt solicited by invisible agents

---

[83] "A curious breeze / A garlic breath / Which sounded like a snore . . .."
Frank Zappa, "Evelyn, a modified dog." To which an anonymous Talmudic
commentator responded: "I think that the garlic breeze and sounded like a
snore might pertain to Garlic yes. and the place called Gilmore California
(the garlic capital of the world) Maybe someone belched by the piano and it
sounded like a snore?"

[84] "The World / has become divided / from the Universe. Put the three Towns /
together". Charles Olson, "Poem 143 The Festival Aspect."

to assure querulous cows the way home
remains straight and broad. Increased
operations to again eliminate once
and for all already eliminated pockets
of resistance hope so too.[85] In that sense hope

is not a time and places are not nothing
to shake a stick at especially if they
are hopeless or at least determined
in their destabilized disinhibatory
vibration polarities to wander outside
the bounds of same laminar aether
coordinates how to do it in unified theory
applications field errant razz eruptions
and sudden unprogrammed Tootie displays
into images of singularly bright
and toothsome estimations of imminent victory

---

[85] See "Ongoing operations to eliminate all pockets of resistance minus one,"
Michael Boughn, *SubTractions: opus minus one.*

Canto 34 – Pollution of distances

One-eyed sheepherders are often less likely
to draw to an inside arrangement
of heroic anticipatory lexical formations
given the encompassing arenas of distance
claiming stakes marked out in monstrous
perspectives narrowing escape routes'
branching deliria into constricted exits

Constricted exits indicate conclusive
apparati arrangements have been instilled[86]
and the way out rendered a pollution of distant
hopes being sorted and stacked into walled
enclosures seen to waver in particulate
atmospheres. The waver may be a sign
indicating conditional release or the edge

of a *veritas* field claiming certain unwobbling
pivotal stakes as therapeutic in the light
of same old dwindling polis solution
enclosed and terminated by the Lords
of Progress and corporate sheep farmers.
The body of ungulate animus toward
all things deviating from narrowing points

of arrival indicates foreclosure
of dual momentum into non-negotiable
spatial slabs.[87] Wonder evacuates
the premises pursued by howls of laughter

---

[86] "Humanism is a secular religion thrown together from decaying scraps of Christian myth." John Gray, *Straw Dogs*.

[87] Alberti gives background on the principles of geometry, and on the science of optics. He then sets up a system of triangles between the eye and the object viewed which define a visual pyramid. He gives a precise concept of proportionality which determines the *apparent* size of an object in the picture relative to its actual size and distance *from the observer*. This slab of observer centered space exists to contain the human.

emanating in conical sections from across
the hall. But all attempts to render
possible extensions of distant adumbrations'

confrontational clarities are disputed
by lyrical wave functions locking
down locutional proliferations
into arrangements suitable for the CBC[88]
or various display case publication
constructions designed to provide
comfort and reassurance to wavering

senses of formerly untroubled claims
on singular integrated modes of spatial
possession. The distances go underground
maliciously constituting non-retrogradable
nations of nothing but pluribus variances,
dilating the dark toward terrific exigencies
of contingent cloaca evacuations.

---

[88] The Canadian Broadcasting Corporation.

Canto 35 – The natural sequence of ideas

The untimely issue of expelled interpretations
rises skyward. No unseemly or patched
interrogations escape. The approaching margin
may be cause for alarm. Circuitous
passages to the contrary probably indicate
sudden ideas. In the event this fails
stay calm and assign optional trajectories.

Beginning again belongs outside
former sequences' constellation of hilarity.
In the unlikely case excessive laughter
leads to sequential insertions of bizarre
objects, inextendible paths backwards
have been known to harbour judges
who may find plaintive lyrics in order.

What follows beyond the pale of extreme
judicial contractions once again reaffirms
the truth of fiction as it exposes unlikely
prolix diversions into imaginary gardens
where adjectives are largely discouraged. No
further deviations are visible in circumcised
oracular eye jobs. They just rise up

against serial darkness's irregular howling
and seek asylum in periodic sentences. Grammatically
the outcome cannot be contained
in subordinate clauses' polar implications
given foreclosure of acknowledgement
every sharp is already always a flat. Beginning
on a different note is frowned upon

by Trotskyite poets from the hills eschewing
badges in places whose time may have come
upon inexplicable but strangely concupiscent
breaches. They gape asunder but nothing

further ranges beyond treasured mother
lode as they drift through dreams
of perfectible dawns. Inordinate

predictions of unnatural pairings
rattle future accounts bearing
interested parties aloft and threatening
singular assertions of nature's all
too facile sequential fantasies
with methodical disintegration[89]
and arbitrary sodomite lexical positions.

---

[89] "Truth is the appearance of being – the resplendence of Proust's buttercups,
Caravaggio's illuminated rationality – rather than a conceptualizable 'secret'
of being. In a sense, there is nothing "to know," only the consciousness of
the movement in which we participate." Leo Bersani, *Caravaggio's Secrets*.

Canto 36 – The Invisible Hand of the Market

Slipped calibrations of ontological severity
stripped of all zing[90] and duded up to resemble

baroque filigreed manipular immensity
determinations that turned Tootie into a pale

version of former dimensional inversion
ruptures[91] often led to happy assertions

of limit's giddy ascension on time's
calculated wing claiming connection

to some long ago art project. The moving
finger writ and having bit off more

than a few filial implications boldly
signifies mandated determinations

of selected freedom functions and
inscriptions along the lines of *Adamo*

me fecit as an antidote to terror
of compassion compulsions and eventual

loss of digital dexterity beyond framed
bonum impositions gussied up

in white robes and carrying fully loaded
harps. Corporate dematerialization

---

[90] As we have no immediate experience of what other men feel, we can form
no idea of the manner in which they are affected, but by conceiving what we
ourselves should feel in the like situation." Adam Smith, *The Theory of Moral
Sentiment*.

[91] "To the Vegetated Mortal Eye's perverted and single vision | The Bellows
are the Animal Lungs, the Hammer, the Animal Heart, | the Furnaces, the
Stomach for Digestion." William Blake, *Jerusalem* 3:14-16.

reaches out[92] straining after some new Adam
Smith to anoint with infinite bounty

reserved for Elect investment bankers
and inside traders by majestic beclouded

instance's archonic transformation[93]
of unpolluted distances characteristic

non-specific points of departure[94] into fixed
exchanges of near and far offered at discounted

fares[95] along with cancellation insurance's
guaranteed promise of risk-free descent

into palm-lined boulevards unobstructed
access to endless fetching points of purchase.

---

[92]"I cannot live under pressures from patrons, let alone paint." Michelangelo, quoted in Vasari's *Lives of the Artists*

[93]"On account of the reality of the authorities, (inspired) by the spirit of the father of truth, the great apostle - referring to the 'authorities of the darkness' - told us that 'our contest is not against flesh and blood; rather, the authorities of the universe and the spirits of wickedness.' I have sent this (to you) because you inquire about the reality of the authorities." The Hypostasis of the Archons.

[94]"*zama zama ōzza rachama ōza,*" *Pistis Sophia*, tr. G. R. S. Mead.

[95] "The mind is a marketplace . . . .." John Barr, President and CEO of PoetryUSA, Inc.

BOOK 7

DE BINARES NATURA

Canto 37 – Waiting for the train

It leaps out like that across the gap's
yawning electrified annunciation

of the two of them stretching the eye
toward some distant Renaissance trick

continues to lower expectations even as it
swings the works into vibratory state

generating derazzified formulae
of instant constitution corralled

into flight from three's licentious
seductive promise of damp paradaisal

intimations undoes end of the line's
distant contract with tomorrow.[96]

The cows cross it at their own risk
declaring autonomous intentions

at designated level crossings
accompanied homeward bound

by many friends and relatives
hell bent on wreaking flagrant

misnomers on passing indications
of restless or unstable salutations

beyond the normal kind.[97] The normal
kind are not abnormal, not

---

[96] "It is because the world undergoes itself as a world of separation that its experience takes the form of the "self." Jean Luc Nancy, *Homo Sacer*.

[97] "We'll let Teisias and Gorgias continue sleeping. For they noticed that plausible stories win more public honour than the truth." Plato, *Phaedrus* 267a6.

different than the cows when they're
friendly, and they smell better, too.

But mostly it's the knowledge
of doing good, real good, the kind

that carries a big weapon to deal
righteously with lascivious mediations

and other aberrations of invariable
distance's arrangement of the furniture[98]

into decent formations suitable
for god-fearing cows on their way home.

[98]"For the same letter denotes sky, sea, earth, rivers, sun, the same denote
crops, trees, animals." Lucretius, *De Rerum Natura* 2: 1015-17.

Canto 38 – Electrified annunciation

Getting our feet down on the ground
slapping mud was no mean trick, vanishing

or not. Certain aerial outlooks may result
in vertiginous intermezzos but

there's something to be said for tree top
dreams of unlikely impervious placations

as long as discounted *porne* haunts
don't rise up wraith like and wrathful

leaving you dangling by sacrificial
implications.[99] Then tracks may indicate

animal presences bolstered by bad acts
and judicious divisions. But brought

to earth leaves heaven dangling by a proverb
hooked up to indicate acceptable points

of contact[100] maintain distances approved
as grounded in properly established codes

of wired practices bent on eliminating
threats tubal detritus bequeaths in walled

recollections of yesteryear's potentially
saleable grace droppings.[101] Still, toe to toe

---

[99] "*Homo sapiens*, then, is neither a clearly defined species nor a substance; it is, rather, a machine or device for producing the recognition of the human." Giorgio Agamben, *The Open*.

[100] "Paleolithic man, however, was long accustomed to living in caves. Hills are not only more secure, they're nearer to heaven." *God's Wand*.

[101] "The Word is the sound of the block's shuttle. The name of the block means 'creaking of the word.'" Ogatamelli.

does exceed singular translations *reductio*
by several magnitudes of stellar residue

and though no refereed outcome remains
tantalizingly beyond any permitted charge

to the contrary, better living through indecent
and unregulated polar remissions still holds out

some promise of connectivity beyond electrified
annunciation warnings to remain on designated

platforms while massive engines of anticipated
and already determined lines of eager

acceleration ride down rails all dolled up
as great steaming hulks of terminal thought.[102]

---

[102] "Has anybody heard from the Institute? / Has anybody seen worn corduroy
soft and mellow / In the warm mountain sun? Has anybody heard?" Gilbert
Sorrentino, "The Institute Doesn't Answer."

Canto 39 – Distant vanishing tricks

Those retrogradable institutions of higher
speculation stretching toward bifocal

limit's electrified annunciation of spatial
argument's endless quibbling leave

no room for Buzz Corey to maneuver
making for dehydrated trajectories

and fixed polar orientations ossified gyroscopic
fundament.[103] Razz, having made way

through compulsory negative obligatory
enclosure functions and reached escape

velocity releases life lines[104] in the shape
of asyntactic assemblages of random

vocables dashing wildly through shadows
seeking succor from their dark, sweet

teats. The Vanishing Point in pursuit
issues proclamations to the contrary rendering

all possible avenues of egress into
culminations of well-lit purification

techniques. Antithetical authorizations
attempt to gather disclosed spatial

---

[103] "That's one of the tragedies of this life, that the men who are most in need of a beating, are always enormous." John D. Hackensacker III (Rudy Vallee), "The Palm Beach Story."

[104] "The grit | of things, | a measure | resistant . . .". Robert Creeley, "Song."

terminations into nets capable of corralling Buzz[105]
as he enters here through a worm hole

from a previous poem actually written
after this. Distance shudders and time

emits weak desperate declarations
of correspondence hoping filial adumbrations

can withstand hard knocks and gleeful
disrespect emanating counter clock

wise from undeclared extensions
of non-parallel hoochy koochy matrix

functions known to shred carefully decorated
elaborations of never the twain etcetera.[106]

---

[105] "The colonizing tendency of Christianity is echoed in the attempts of
    Galilean, Cartesian, and Newtonian physics to appropriate whole realms
    formerly consigned to alchemy and 'natural philosophy' not to mention
    local customs and history." Edward Casey, *The Fate of Place*.
[106] "Holy smokin' rockets, commander!" Space Cadet Happy, *Space Patrol*.

Canto 40 – Aberrations of invariable distance

As a state of mind founded somewhere
near the southern border where fabled

Razza'ma rose from the marshes, its
curved walls bending space to the grace

of their jubilation and governed by errant
insertions of unexpected derationalizing relish

it hovers near an horizon bonds earth
to sky in aberrant variation's formerly

mashed extrusions of inadequate
consideration.[107] Considering possible tracks'

indeterminate assimilations of hazy
conclusions only leads to further

perfunctory estimations of Vanishing
Point's insatiable appetite for terminal

buildings tastefully located in orderly
extensions of democracy. The hordes

who are gathered and placed in postures
signifying gratitude, right hand raised

pointer extended into cerulean
intimations of paradaisal choices beyond

the next town fall into hushed tones
of ahhh generally reserved for victorious

---

[107] "The bead of light that emerges from our defects and our little abjections is
nothing other than redemption." Giorgio Agamben, "The Assistants."

groups of cows as they cross the Finishing
Line, patting its butt in unrepressed

testament to glutteal admiration.
The Finishing Line, also known as Phil,[108]

indicates its pleasure by quickly banning
proliferating aberrations on grounds

infiltration undermined with impermissible
variations of gradation's distance

from invariably held belief in no further filiations
upholds truth's firm manipular emissions.

---

[108] Any resemblance here, however remote, to scandalous suggestions of un-
natural and unseemly conjunctions of philanthropy, philately, and philoso-
phy should be considered purely and solely the result of overindulgence in
illegal substances and gross, unregulated lexical irresponsibility.

Canto 41 – End of the line

Is it the thought of no final exit
other than that looming inevitable dark

kiss that separates the rails into vanishing
trick instigates formations of human

declaratory spatial impositions limiting
chiaroscuro eruptions to decidedly

predictable patterns of singular solar
contract mechanisms, binding Razz

and Tootie back to back?[109] On the one hand
is the end of a line. On the other insists

variations are merely fluctuating instances
of magnetic proton alignment's temporary

loss of precious bodily fluids. Getting
there abrogates undetermined meetings

to small dark spaces pop up from time
to time trailing clouds of atemporal

flotsam in the shape of triangular
vibrating intrusions leading to further

irregular assignation's surplus
itineraries and sloppy exclamations

of mutual arrival. In and out is no
mere aleatory *interruptus*, but a genuine

---

[109] "The curtain is turned back, | old man losing flesh | within the grim crucial percussion, | lying beside a photocopy of winter. | Or is it that I love you, my falcon | while instead you restore me | to my own gainful sovereignty, flesh?" Asa Benveniste, "Short Scene Sonnets xi," *Pommes Poems.*

assertion of possible combinatory
copulas propensity to pile on propitious

piquancy[110] in the face of cows on their way
toward some distant vanishing trick's

nostalgic incursion. The path to madness
step by step exfoliates through logic's

certain adumbrations into endless aisles
of toiletries arranged to excite blood

flows into impossible architectures
of separation hung out on lines to dry.

---

[110] Occasional, unpredictable eruptions of overdetermined, egregious poetic
language are often due to uncontrollable lapses in the Pathtic Fellatio rather
than attempts to satisfy editors demands for intensity of the first order and
authentic and interesting expressions. The author denies any ontological
status.

Canto 42 – Lascivious mediations

Intervention inhales frequently though always
between sheets of immaculate
irregularities' untoward estimations

of involuntary signification contractions.[111]
If it feels good does the proposition lose
angular incidence and authentic bovine

directional modus? The void skulking
just around the last corner shifts
in shadows rattling the dented lid

of a garbage can suddenly spooking
a black cat darts over the ragged fence
in moonlight.[112] Now the stage is set

for razzle dazzle lexical assignations
behind pebbled-glass paned door
opens into chiaroscuro foliations.[113] Tootie

snaps down the brim of her hat anticipating
pencil thin destiny's sap to the back
of some unlikely train of thought only

to find Razz, sleek, firm nylon
smooth gams crossed, smoke gently
rising past veiled suggestions of cheap

---

[111] ". . . what fell from the borders of ether, that is again brought back, and the regions of heaven again receive it." Lucretius, *De Rerum Natura* 2:1002-1004.

[112] "What a place. I can feel the rats in the walls." Jack Marlow (Franchot Tone), *Phantom Lady.*

[113] "I saw a broken down piece of machinery. Nothing but the buck, the bed and the bottle for the rest of my life. That's what I saw." Kelly (Constance Towers), *The Naked Kiss.*

hotel room's flickering neon
paradise. Outraged on the other
hand squeals to the Vanishing

Point about lowdown lascivious
mediations in the local flop house quickly
mobilizing intentional acts of self

validating authenticity to batter down
the door to the last century releasing
various mounted formations to mow down

the nick of time in the interest of self
preservation and general control
of potentially intoxicating agents

of provocative non sequiturs hell bent
on breeding lilacs out of whatever vociferant
dung heap vocabulary tickles their dirty roots.[114]

---

[114] "Pieces of the past arising out of the rubble. Which evokes Eliot | and then
evokes Suspicion. Ghosts all of them. Doers of no | good. | The past around
us is deeper than. | Present events defy us, the past | Has no such scruples."
Jack Spicer, *Six poems for Poetry Chicago.*

BOOK 8

PANCAKES

He shakes my ashes
greases my griddle,
churns my butter,
strokes my fiddle,
my man is
such a handy man.

– Ethel Waters

Canto 43 – AJ discourses on the cosmic egg

Ain't no two ways about it whatever
their directions dictate and inextendible
paths backward don't count for beans

in Orphic misprisions through
proliferating strings of song and
dancing stones unlikely ascent into exact

unique forms of wiggle logic[115] recalled
from illimitable depths of egg's
imperishable groove. Turn around

and face the music while you still
got the legs leaves otherwise relegated
to mere business of exaggerated

restrictions known to elevate
likely codas beyond means music itself
exists within[116] and rendered pale

by excited enjambments' daring
return trips deep into stories
determined descending flapjack

increments escape from yoked imperatives
upward gaze toward perfectly
balanced satisfactions while emergent

hog calling intimations stumble beyond
egghead abstractions into scrambled
oeuvre's unanticipated *concilia*

---

[115] "Once the band starts, everybody starts swaying from one side of the street
to the other, especially those who drop in and follow the ones who have
been to the funeral. These people are known as 'the second line' and they
may be anyone passing along the street who wants to hear the music. The
spirit hits them and they follow." Louis Armstrong.

[116] " . . . 'beauty' is related not to 'loveliness' but to a state in which reality
plays a part." William Carlos Williams, *Spring & All.*

imperative.[117] Bound ingredients
from coagulating head over heels
obligato busting out wail

rising high and fine from atop walls
of fabled Razza'ma tumble into broken
paeans to delta openings[118] cloven

hot stacks and waiting secrets of a dark
sweet oracle leading up and out
to sit amid piles of sticky glories.

---

[117] "It seems that the human mind has first to construct forms independently
before we can find them in things." Albert Einstein.

[118] "It is the voice of the line | coming from that dark place | to foreshadow
in | a foreground | our eyes are not yet | accustomed to; | these sentences
about whose | syntactical connections | we are told nothing." Stephen Jonas,
Morphogenesis.

Canto 44 – AJ discourses on the milk of kindness

Sometimes you'd think the dancing
stones had up and relocated themselves
to various infernal cavities inhabiting
proprioceptive determinations' heart
variations.[119] Then they up and start

howling living intimations
of unanticipated organic bubble seeds
laying awake through all that space
bearing messages of further
implicate pulse sometimes even sets your

feet to tapping.[120] The cow's involvement
is timely but transitory, two deflections
of razzamatootie into determined telic
saturations' single minded pursuit
of soft posteriors presenting ineffable

suggestive images of Tootie promise
tied up in plodding inertial satieties
one hoof after another. Udder folly[121]
can wreak havoc on all manner
of *domus* determined inversions even

---

[119] "They'd just as soon sell ya | a poison pizza as look atcha. || They'd Just as soon fireya | as hireya. || And they'd rather | killya than feedya." Ed Dorn, "These Times Are Medieval."

[120] "Organic bubbles that could serve as dwellings for primitive life have been discovered inside a space rock that fell to Earth nearly three years ago.. . . Other research by various groups has provided some evidence to support a bolder speculation involving space rocks, that they actually might have delivered life itself to our planet. One study showed that life from Mars, if it ever existed, could have been transported to Earth inside a rock, thus making us all descendents of early Martians." Robert Roy Britt. See also Jack Spicer on Martians, i.e. "Yeah. But my answer to playing tricks on the Martians is a poem by Ogden Nash. It's a lovely two-line poem: "When called by a panther / Don't anther." Jack Spicer, Interview with Warren Tallman. Which may or may not be relevant to the following footnote.

[121] "The cow is of the bovine ilk; | One end is moo, the other, milk." Ogden Nash, "The cow."

when they're dished up cold with ketchup
and the stones' further possibilities implode
in the face of impenetrable expectations'
non-designated resolutions.[122] When it goes
south all manner of stuff curdles at the top

opening eternal instant's inhabitable
modus variations to prescriptions
of best before cylindrical determinants
non-negotiable discard demands. A waste
of time[123] if you ask me, hon, generated

by knee jerk disposable declensions
too distant from hand to mouth
or even basic end of the week
box roust to know the difference
a day makes is often little more than

slight swelling among lactational apparati
render mouth watering, lip puckering
milk and honey visions no handy man ever
mistook for anything other than intimations
of rising frenzy's come hither tremendum.[124]

---

[122] "Now, for what the world thinks of that ejaculation – I would not give a groat." Laurence Sterne, *Tristram Shandy,* Vol. IX chapter IX.

[123] "I want a slow and easy man | He needn't ever take the lead | Cause I work on that long-time plan | And I ain't a-lookin' for no speed." Ida Cox, "One hour Mama blues."

[124] "The Authors are in eternity. | Our eyes reflect | prospects of the whole radiance | between you and me . . .." Robert Duncan, "Variations on Two Dicta of William Blake."

Canto 45 – AJ discourses on wheat and chaff

What's blowing in the wind has
altered considerably since ringing
air rallied instance's broken promises

to protestant variations of ordinary
transformations and foot tapping
razz impulsion to catch a gust

rise up and wiggle your heart out.[125]
Mitigating cross breezes whip the air
into more engaging articulations

of discriminating tendency's inevitable
breath of fresh expectation beyond
strong expressions of lyric intensity's

prize laden recipe for stable formations
of contented cows.[126] Pancakes is
as pancakes does registers recalcitrant

economies of rising hilarity's electrical
neuro-logos spasm directives leave
the VP looking for some corner to hang

it's hat and set up shop turning out
obsolescent imprecations against non-standard
spatial variances known to open peculiar

---

[125] "Everything must become food. The art of drawing life out of everything.
To vivify everything is the goal of life. Pleasure is life. The absence of
pleasure is a way to pleasure, as death is a way to life." Novalis, "Logological
Fragments 1."

[126] "By which I imagine what I mean is that if the grass that is not real is real,
as it undoubtedly is, what would be the difference between the way grass
that is not real is real and the way real grass is real, then?" David Markson,
Wittgenstein's Mistress.

conversations between lines of bound
projections.[127] The rules ain't the game,
hon, and the spaces between will always

trump the likely separation railing
against slippery slopes sure fire
pollution of distances' claim to

undifferentiated demeanors of decorous
discontent's[128] cover story into full bore
hoochy koochy equivocations. Equity

in this unexpected vocation generates
division driven gusts having no
relation to known instances of infernal

affairs as outlined in manuals to the contrary
but affiliates idylls of separation into recipes
for unforeseen husk evacuations.

---

[127] "You open that window again, I'll throw you out of it." Alec Stiles (Richard
    Widmark), *The Street with No Name*.
[128] Another eruption of the Pathetic Fellatio. Cf. Book 7, Canto 41.

Canto 46 – AJ discourses on katastematic pleasures

Ten dollar words won't get you far
in this neck of inscrutable intimations
but wine dark deposits of unstable

satisfactions can go a long way
toward instigating post-Tootie
exuberance mediations and extensions

of *three* beyond decent folks' negative
declarations and *porne* renunciations
all dolled up as illusions of glory

incursions from sad-assed backyards
of last season's prize winning garden
gone to hell in a market-basket.[129] Give me

that old time teeter-totter in your face
ecstasis and I'll give you one damn fine
party, hon, when all that even keel

business is starting to look around
for a way out of Epicurean Chinese
handcuffs looking to lock up

the old twiddle factor and keep the flow
slow, Joe, it's a damn shame and that old
morning after throb somewhere near

cerebellum's link up to higher as the say
points of currently malfunctioning
clarification *apparati* painful as it

---

[129] "He's got to get it, bring it, and put it right here | Or else he's gonna keep it out
there | If he must steal it, beg it, or borrow it somewhere | Long as he gets it, I don't
care." Bessie Smith, "Put it right here blues."

continues to be is no reason to avoid
uncontrolled burgeoning *ecstasis* novas
fueled by whatever poison fires up

the old engine.[130] Getting down
to business don't add up to much more
than interstitial signal contaminants

hijacked by alien meaning pirates
hell bent on turning flap jacks' consensual
conversion factor into contractual

assertability conditions leave between
high and dry, bereft of lubricious
deviations' slip-slide long stack spasm.

---

[130] "There's a party in my mind, | and I hope it never stops." Talking Heads,
"Memories Can't Wait."

Canto 47 – AJ takes a break

It's a known fact all them big words
will give you a swoon just swirling
around like some bad ass mixer

cut loose and run amok in Tootie's unsecured
word horde, whipping up concatenations
of juicy syllabic unliklihood and spraying

them across the wall in *mene mene tekel*
apparitions of insect reason yearning
after Lucretian eruptions of multiphonic

aural infestation.[131] Roll over and light a smoke
reeks of irreducible residue's appeal to moment's
sweet profanity.[132] And no museum can hold

its impromptu rush through memory's tidal
push and pull, that wet grind, or bind
its suddenly recovered use to a spectacle

of committee approved displays guaranteed
to please the countless tourists having flown
in for the weekend to gaze longingly

at large groups of cows dressed
in native costumes and lifting their hooves
in good old down home bovine hoedown

expressions of felicitous antelope infestations
and encouraging exclamations regarding
lower prices. A huge sigh of relief

---

[131] "who gauges the shadow games? || I reek I reek | of *mimologique*." Gerrit
Lansing, "The Soluble Forest 2."

[132] "Every man, philosopher included, ends in his own finger-tips." D.H.
Lawrence

has been known to frequent disreputable
disputations on the occasions of sudden
interruptions recalling violet skies

through windows streaked beyond
acceptable limits of accumulated
swing leaves the whole joint

approaching the speed of slightly
miscued diversions.[133] Shattering
land records spill across broken

sound and recurring split infinities
rendering gaps in the work day
incompatible with uncontested thoughts

of tonic resolution's leisurely after
math and complete sentences leading
the garden path into indefinite

distance's predatory consecration[134] amid
instances implying sudden relief
from barren insistence on wholesome nuances.

---

[133] "I'd walk six miles | out of my way | To hear again | the slow decay | Of that
piano | far away -- || King Tubby's | Studio A." Peter Culley, "Paris 1919."

[134] "In its extreme form the capitalist religion realizes the pure form of separa-
tion, to the point there is nothing left to separate. An absolute profanation
without remainder coincides with equally vacuous and total consecration."
Giorgio Agamben, "In Praise of Profanation."

Canto 48 – AJ discourses on syrup

Corn's got its uses but never for a minute
confuse it with that boiled down tree blood
that's not just sweet but fit to drizzle

over any hot little lexical consensus
rises up steaming though not averse
to instance's frequent recourse to release

mechanisms known to leave various
cascading words in states of sticky
residue as a sign of Tootie's shameless

and insatiable quest to evade specific
claim to exhausted exigencies nominal
cramping. Swallows would like to dart

through it again[135] but at this precarious
point finds its parameters restricted
to ingestional contractions following

lip smacking. Smacking your lips around that
may result in accidents without substance
proliferating beyond evaporating images

put into play precisely in the impossibility
of this having been written.[136] No radio
ever had it so revocably clear as that sticky

outcome's amber imbrication makes
evident to the pure of heart leaving
by the back door after having snatched

---

[135] cf. Book 1 Canto 1.

[136] "Without narrative as background, as well as 'limit' which is gravity itself,
images of identity cluster only in statistical distribution, leaving the primacy
of recognition bound to what seems like minimum entropy in the immedi-
ate foreground; not a good substitute for the negentropy of either art or
life." John Clarke, *From Feathers to Iron*, Book 4.

hoochy koochy equivocations from jaws
of victory's inevitable ritual celebration
dressed to the nines but having exchanged

Miss Emily's lowly interrogation[137] for self
satisfied ascensions along prescribed
lists of national reading. That is no way

to treat a long hot stack just begging
for it. Abandoned terminals leave no
possible arrival other than climactic

contractions fading into difficult extractions
and diverted hopes for constitutional
invention's yet to be determined issue.

---

[137] "I am Nobody! Who are you? – Are you – Nobody – too – ?"

BOOK 9

DIVERTED DIVAGATIONS

*". . . a movement is absolute when, whatever its
quantity and speed, it relates one, or 'a' body considered
as multiple, to a smooth space that it occupies in the
manner of a vortex."*
– Gilles Deleuze

Canto 49 – Meandering

Modes of transport often lost in frankly
non-variable telic *domus* visions'
vanishing trick imperative lead to

delusional anti-Walden fixations
implicated in antiphonal contretemps
known to be previously determined

in temporal spatial regulations establishing
maximal t, s, and d predictabilities
as part of the whole package

of Razz containment. No hurry leads
to severe eruptions of lop-sided differences
leave even Buzz Corey wondering which

way is not so much up as just indicative
of space patrol's prerogative to proceed
without being bound to gravitational

terminations of every which way and loose
to boot. The way unfolds by means
as yet unspecified in official manuals

of eddy interruption and backwater
formations eluding movement
quantifications and manifesto gunk

deposits. Relief ripples through arching
passage's vague, leafy shadow
intimations in stippled vault

bound light bars spilling unseemly
old chaoses across sudden banks
of mistranslated effabilities. Then

you're nearly there, as if it hadn't always
known you were indistinguishable
from shadows. Wave function impositions

may waver and collapse into grateful
cats whose tracks leave the box rendering
unrecognizable vanishing insinuations

of formerly ambiguous proposals
into voluptuous resolutions and barn-door
closing celebrations while somewhere

rumours of indicative harmonization
necessities evaporate slowly, gaseous
residue of countless old elevation

measures dissipating in intricate paths
cross and recross morning sky in careless
abjurations of ever getting there.

Canto 50 – Roving

Streaming along unconcerned
with riparian terminations is no limit
to syntactical blossoming – raving
is unconcerned, too, and may yet claim
to represent a concurrent equivocation

slipping between surprised syllables
as though it could actually get you
there, even as obligations to sweeping
increments accrue along lines of hopeful
flight and sudden brazen reversals lead
quickly past lyric warbles toward marauding

possibilities and surprise raids
on bordering states of mind. Starting
over with original calculations of hollowed
out alternatives may mean getting there
quicker, though it doesn't help stabilize
resulting sums nor does there have any

more discriminate claim on your
anticipated deflections. *Au contraire*
may figure at the heart of it, especially
in the presence of full, blank invitations
to try another turn if you can catch it.
What lurks there often forgets not only
what's come before but how to signal

the sense intense amours may require
as part of a gay but passing encounter.
Returning to the lintel hell-bent
on encounters staggering out of eternity
intersecting negentropic excursions
into hostile circumstances extenuated

beyond decent limits satisfactory expulsion
of familiar strangeness leaves the sentence
with nowhere to go. Aleatory horizons
roil with shadows tracing hands on heaven
grasping nothing – hi, I'm here – while
itinerant bands of carnal determination

hoot from the sidelines waving banners
with Gordian pleasures newly imposed
penetrations depicted in bold but simple
strokes. The waste laid to wholesome
interpretations leaves therapeutic
dispensations on hands and knees begging

for more. Seeing no cure can find its text
in such predictable vocabularies, viral
misprisions cut loose, galloping through
morphemic projections six shooters
blazing, wreaking havoc on cows
stampeding through streets of home.

Canto 51 – Drifting

Aerial impulsions regarding unmoored
implications toward wayward assignations
may lead to controlled catastrophes, pie
theft and fluvial ambitions. There's no

telling unanticipated gusts and surreptitious
glances into dipping revelations of cloven
moment's soft promise to behave when rules

of engagement were already rewritten
before the current running through bloody

disturbances beyond bounds decency
always wants to erect around them
were determined in laboratories discontinuous

flows left behind long ago. There rises
and then catching a gust loses track
of incessant chatter hard on its trail,

disturbing the getting, leaving it clutching
after ennui provocations deadly aim
at intensity's always interesting arrangements
of already over, already turned out

on bleak corners to strut its stuff before
leaving memories of good old authentic

devotion to finding slightly over grown paths
and extraordinary extenuations of standard

trajectory's mode of transport. While
it may look uncomfortable, it never
lacks for direction, terminal satisfaction's
enormous collection of 18th century
first editions, and plush chairs

fully funded for tarting up avant
gardes deemed of salacious potential

for the English Department of the Soul.
Washing up on discordant beaches

may result in smoother insinuations
but ultimately direct transmission
of bottled signage suffers interruptions.

Then it's just grey quilted passage over

lines of mass intent and directed fears'
outrage at assumptions of abandoned hand

in hand through noble if perilous proposals
regarding real feelings that never need
explanation, validated and stamped
by participating merchants seeking traffic
through furniture's congested erections.

Canto 52 – Blundering

Unexpected entrances into passages reeking
of bad taste often compromise even
devoted instabilities. Inexcusable repetitions
render them fodder for egregious translations
into fallacious resemblances to poetry
previously established in defense of overdone

erections trussed up for the holidays. You
never know what gawdawful combination
of unintentional retorts will find their way
into stories of carnal anxieties' wars
of dubious intent. The rising death toll shreds
protestations of democratic vistas inevitable

remedy for what ails you. Too late for love's
yearly eruption to do more than guarantee
profitable annual terminations. Anyway, they
don't look like they come from Dallas, leaving
dusky roots to spread beyond wordy genetic
urgencies. Tripping is then a tactical contingency

under circumstances dictated more
by mental shortcomings dazzled
by nifty blueprints for perfectly executed
finales than deep binding with other
paths past brain locks looking a lot like
Virgilian paradise dumps hidden

in long grass. Stepping in one of those
tenders pastoral affections in shades
of lingering emissions like some errant
if insidious serendipity clinging to pedal
extremities stinking of nature's insistent
resolution into squishy excretions'

reminder of telic dreams illusory wind up
in CBC grade moral declamations.
Blind to abruptly broken joint is no
excuse for unseemly elegance. Clumsily suddenly
figures a way out is not just dazzling
but dependent on diversionary adumbrations

and multiple unresolved mortality
encounters. It doesn't add up stumbles
into reassuring annunciations of forth
coming redemptive architectural investments
soothing the waters. And sudden walls
can be a problem, especially when dazzled

fallen from the arms of Razz renders
further blank if not null, though some
have been known to wind up in percolating
extensions and boogie apparitions
depending how the bones tumble
and fall and tumble in the big black bowl.

Canto 53 – Wandering

When the beginning lost its end
Pelasgian metaphysics registered a state
of affairs irresistible to lines of least
intrusive motivations which

no doubt shine with the light
particular to vagrant powers ignorant
of multitasking. Purpose enters
in spite of the ignorance. Boulevards

and arcades then abound, unreeling
precise arches and leafy corridors
in invitations to further extrapolations
seeking to evade interpretation. There's no

telling Eurynomic avatars which way
is loose when every way holds out new
encounters with unusable material designated
unprofitable for polite company. Somewhere

near the end beckons, blushing, mounting
excitement in a public display of unanticipated
equestrian affection. But no beckoning
figures beyond the sudden apparition of another

corner. Turning there is a matter best left
there as the moment splits and the sea breaks
against the turning. It is a choice
the next corner contests and the brouhaha

unseemly as a predictable metaphor abusing
the ocean with its uses, disperses, turning,
leaving obliquities to morph into virtual
obligatos refusing to condense supersaturated

images into chronic fixation's abjuration
of the perpetual infinitive. To rises
from the ashes of issues returning
moment to the door that opens on yet

another internecine impertinence scattered
over the Riemann Hills in unrecognizable
rhythmic grotesqueries. Passing through
the lintel initiates post-Lucretian configurations

of composing incandescence but does not
indicate which way the car is going,
the goddamn big one whose ambiguous
drive just hangs there forever in first light

its wings spread against the memory
of surging air, unwilling to clarify devotional
demands insistent whine when every which
way sings a further dappled dawn

Canto 54 – Gallivanting

Razzamatootie deviations leading
to untoward expectations count

as incentives to engage lexical assignations
in awkward postures that may increase

stimulation and lead to explosive moments'
determined evasion of measured paces. It's

not just for the fun of it either. Muddy cloaks
linger in ravaged echoes of royal feet, vulgar

puddles, and rolling heads bobbing
with other detritus on the murky water

beyond lost memories gallant garment's
regal pedal salvation misplaced along

with tobacco in cans and Roanoke.[138] Other
bobbings have been known to yield multiplicities

of amorous salivation too. No mere rump
apparition, but genuine celestial atavism

yielding unregulated repetition formations
in prophetic postures of evaporating peach

cleft redemption. Then the cloak reenters
virtually indistinguishable from the night

sky all over town inviting us to step
high and fine into the sudden music

---

[138] The only clue to their fate was the word "CROATOAN" and letters "CRO" carved into separate tree trunks.

piping somewhere in the distance. Tearing
open the firmament, salvage operations

emerge from the puddle making way
for the dawn before the dawn. Anorganic

intuitions begin to become Fred as limned
by leaking light in the abrupt sky, a stair

a star, or even a stunt hoof around
in embryonic compositional vagaries

of larval disintegration while gallant
gestures undone leave the Royal Foot

awash in the muck of night. The joke is on
the house, rollicking in its evasive

resemblance to canned pranks liberated
into whatever's after the end no one

remembers. Let him out, let him out, it cries
while the skies gathering into portentous aberrations

of inviolable hilarity trip the light fandango
through puddled dark and smoke hole glories.

BOOK 10

UNANTICIPATED
REST STOPS

Canto 55 – Wonderland

Warnings to avoid rabbit holes
rarely go unnoticed though the import
is known to be given to instabilities
and sudden attacks of acute evaporation
seizures when fading felines enter the list
of possible antic opponents. Out of the blue
here you are, blue representing a severe
lack of oxygen or maybe as H.D.
had it, the glow of some itinerant spirit
bearing messages. The messages tend
to propose help is on the way even
as small print qualifications leave
the lurch holding out for any graspable
infusion of oxygen or sudden word
that neither questions, founds, nor
refuses to represent while still managing
a restless form of passage often
mistaken for a sentence till it turns
into a pig and heads for the bush. Help
may resemble infusions of strong
tea or unexpected corners harbouring
nobody known to be a spitting image.
The road is often full of such
encounters. They cry out triggering
gravitational break downs or inordinate
pissant back tracking toward grinning
hope directions may yet transform
cerulean ambiguities into acute asphyxia.

Sudden liquidity of mirrors leaves
each verbal encounter opening into blue
recommendations unnoted
in the original contract. Gasping
for breath the rabbit disappears
around a corner. Then the corner

disappears and only laughter remains, a mere
whiff caught briefly among high bare
branches coated with ice and ablaze
with the sudden memory
of a disclosed star. Not there and there
and not there is what it remembers.
Attenuates leaves the garden
in a huff of unrequited interventionist
dilutions while the star fades
into a grin and is not there. Other
threats indicate royalty's allegiance
to shifting modes of what's always
in the way. The difference spreads
around it leaving puzzled officials
to demand explanations of blue.
But it's not there either and as the pig
sneaks back in resembling an unadorned
equivocation editorial
demands for intensity and the end
to boredom grow louder
in the way of a large grace, flamingo
pink, setting the table just so, though
visions of scattered crocks frolic
in curious pig eyes back from the bush
bearing tales of distant yellow brick roads.

Canto 60 – The O.K. Corral

It's not that you want to end up there
in the haze of smoke with your ears
ringing. It's just that it won't go

away. It could be the cow's thought
of home coincides with formal principles
of enclosure. The violent geometry

exploding out of temporal geode
into broken. Someone pulls a trigger.
The difference a trigger and a rabbit

hole bring to the table leaks all over
the green felt, scattering balls into random
holes, virtually indistinguishable clicks

clicking. The trigger click is also
an encounter of ill repute wrenching
open issues. What emerges may be

considered magic. Why it won't go
away is a kind of magic too. The difference
is not negligible and when they get

to the creek the catastrophe intensifies
leaking clicks beyond striated
anticipations. Hot lead whizzes etching

crystalline temporal stasis out of
moment's flesh. Walking into the flurry
is a kind of magic the enclosure

corrals, turning a man into a verb
before your very eyes. Turning a man
into a verb renders the Clantons

into virtual negations, bushwhackers
risen to an energy level sometimes
confused with Loki. The confusion

indicates successful disruption
of the laminar dream machine's
round up. The cows are not in the corral

when the hot lead flies and heroes
flow through it. Billy, Doc, Virgil, Ike.
The horses are not in the corral too

when biting the dust once again
stretches out to claim a mouth full
of real dirt. The corral is O.K. because

it doesn't get shot and the temporal
stasis is contained while the fallen clamour
in shadow and the others walk into the sun.

Canto 57 – Brigadoon
– *for Al Glover*

The periodic ascension of interdimensional
destiny incursions is not amenable to halogen
fantasies. Fog is a requirement. When it

orbits in its name may be Onetto's
in the right light, Tootie hanging
around in the ruptured distances of strange

alleys and horticultural disturbances flickering
between. Here today tomorrow already
nods off fulfilling fated encounters

with magical flowers disappear in the light
of looking. Out of the fog means some
crumpled space touching the hearts

of vagrant hunters. When they bag one
it points the way beyond the path
toward the fog, though the hunt itself

goes on, almost as if it had a life
of its own devising, a kind of mercurial
unfolding into untold openings

in the fog. Waking up in a fog
may be occasion to break into song
and dance through the heather. The song

is new and the heather resembles
the best the stage manager could do
under circumstances dictated

by today's limited narrative stash.
But when it wakes up, it calls
other stories to it. They all speak

of love as if it was always lost
in the fog and the hunters had passed
it by in the quest for other game

every day for a hundred years.
When it wakes up, it isn't what
it seems. If it's Onetto's

neither are the hunters, and the game
branches into unforeseen pursuits
of strange antlered figures pointing

toward a different matter of fact. Dancing
through the heather can resemble that
even before the fog disappears and the hunters

see it for the first time. It leads them on
and the fog rejoices knowing the return
in the heat of a sudden burning.

Canto 59 – King Solomon's Mines

If they were good enough for Christopher
Columbus and Stewart Granger they're
no doubt still able to rouse expectations
of lingering exegetical excitement
sparkling in cavernous allusions to textual
jewels lurking in dark recesses of interior
moments. Wisdom is no measure

of geographical excitations ability to manifest
hidden earths behind receding layers
of thought. All those jewels must come
from somewhere, even the jewels
that were letters. The spell of encounters
is in the air etching out names. They
are not like smoke, the way they drift

in the air. They are not like stars, the way
they glitter. The jewels glitter across aeons
calling out to Christopher Columbus
and Stewart Granger, though Venezuela
and Zulu country are not known
to usually keep company. When they do
it is in the address to a world of sense

in which guides appear to bind us to cavernous
allusions sparkling in the dark. The guides
may be exiled kings though you wouldn't
know it to look at them. And the spell
of the letters drifts and glitters from the next
poem, beckoning toward unanticipated
rest stops in the perilous jungles or unexpected

islands on the way to the end of the world.
The end of the world glitters and drifts
proposing a vast silence at the other end
of a cave into which plunging renders

the cave itself tumbling. Halving the
proposition leaves wisdom bleeding
when primitive savagery addresses

itself to strange and wild interiors,
calling out in bold letters across
the screen for Riverdale, vast land
of mystery, to watch for the mad charge
of rogue elephants minus the crosshairs.
The persistence of mines lies across
these burning sands which often overlook

drifting and glittering as substantial
signs of unrest break out in grotesque caverns
and sacred dances. Then the promise
of the actual death fight of pagan kings
indicates no further reason but the drift
and glitter beyond the end of the world.

Canto 56 – Oz

Unprecedented phonemic affairs with filing
cabinet alphabet incursions often constitute
yellow brick excursions into lexical
utopian phantasmagoria's open
code. If the wizard's have all gone home

that leaves Dorothy to mind the gap
between here and there, between O and Z
as they circulate through folds of poppies
and straw, courage and high winds. It's not
as if you can actually rest there when antithetical

projections claim your slippers. Worse
you may not even know you are there
when they come for you, dropping out
of a sky given over to a tumult
of indistinguishable darknesses. Every yellow

brick road leads there. Companions
have been known to lurk in the woods
and when they find you uneven deficiencies
render unprecedented phonemes into
occasions for finding avenues of escape

from the rigorous imposition of illusory
interpretations. One place or the other
is not different, even though the monkeys
are meaner. Compensations render
virtual precipitates equal to angle

of shuffled letters transformation
into world's smoke and mirror chorus
behind indigenous screens. Lurking
superfluity in folds of same proves
indifferent is less than it seems, a real

magic, snatching the world while you
sleep and leaving something cold
to greet you when you open your
eyes to the dawn. Then there's no place like
that bar in the Emerald City Dorothy

once frequented, a hangout for tornado
victims and unemployed monkeys,
to remedy the lack of a wizard right when you
need one to pull the wool over eyes
unaccustomed to radical breaches in successful

distinction between here and there. Companions
waver, resembling unstable serendipities'
inability to fulfill promised yellow brick
terminations, leaving The Road belly
up to the bar trying to catch Dorothy's eye.

Canto 58 – Shangri-La

Somehow we always knew the mountains
held secrets. The average trip to school
still saw them. Valleys appear out of the mist
of the secrets. Or through hidden
tunnels. Somehow we always knew

the mountains held tunnels. And that valleys
would wait at the end. Though the tense
may vary, the waiting remains in frosty
air, a cloud of breath hovering. Average
trips to school still saw them around

the sky. They were hovering and the valleys
waited for someone they always knew
would come. Somehow the guide gets
there as you always knew she would. Then
the valley trembles slightly just on the other

side. The hovering breath remains
a kind of promise. Once there frosty air
absconds with the tunnel. Once there
the tunnel is in the mountains and the average
trip to school hovers somewhere else. Somehow

valleys that hovered in the frosty air
always knew you would come though
waiting was necessary as if the promise
was a tunnel cut through the ice
and the secrets glittered within. Then the ice

gives way and the secrets scatter. Old before
their time is the risk of secrets in frosty
tunnels. It always seems to crumble
before the tunnel arrives. This is a secret
and then the pieces blow away, gusts

of frost in the frigid promise valleys
sometimes make. Outside arrives and the pieces
hover in tunnels. Somehow we always knew
gusting secrets would scatter before
the tunnels got there. Hovering

in frigid air the average trip
to school knew secrets would remain
even as the pieces blew away
and the tunnels' horizons scattered
past any thought of the way there beyond

the mountains. Somehow we always hovered
and knew that the way there was no
different. The cold air, the tunnels,
the mountains, somehow we always
knew the way there was different.

BOOK II

DEMONIC VISTAS

Canto 61 – Anthems of indefinite music

"Oh Lord, don't let them drop that atomic bomb on me."
   – C. Mingus

Detours have been known to mislead detritus
into positions compromised by indefinite
function's penchant for dividing the sky

into evasive split infinities, a sign of lapsed
wonder's sliding grip on firm but unfinished
sentence. The remaining time is best

left to its own ends, a trick known to undo
formulations assuring mutual destruction
as a measure of hardened thought

erections horizontal penetration and
proclamations of definite hope. Vague
strains emanate through sudden gaps suggesting

Tootie's imminent return as time draws
to an inside straight then drifts away
in opalescent tattered regalia. In its

wake multiplies, demands for clarity
and intensity rubbing shoulders
with chronos fixations around the table.

The cards fall intervening with airy
digressions in all that forlorn expectation
sometimes known to extricate thought of music's

flesh into distinctly non-carnal
adumbrations' slightly off-white
declarations of exclusively determined

simulations of heavenly encompassing.
The trick is to stand still and listen.
Proliferating similarities

propel indefinite into vague fears
leaking out edges of endless shop
windows, a beyond next to it all

the time, disappointed destinies
beckoning. The trick is to stand still
and listen to it thinking us. Cards come

and go and time returns to the table Tootie
on her arm. Why it's a trick is unstable
and returns anthems from its former

strutting to glad to know you haven't
made it be good, haven't lost jubilant
as a sign of unrestrained lexical

ardor overruling itself with strange
postures of poetic matter arranged
in uneasy geometries of penetration.

Canto 62 – Falling into error again blues

It's hard not to force an opening
when riches shimmer just on the other
hand, though no bilateral arrangement
of perfections has been known to yield

oomph necessary to reach escape
velocity's ragged ass ambition for skies
of unprecedented vacancies. The fact that error
given sufficient syllabic intervention almost

rhymes with prayer is irrelevant
to current ascent into unregulated
discriminations of insignificant
vocal ejaculations where it's well-known

you're on your own. Hence reappearance
of blue which reeks with suggestions
of a theme while slyly evading
artistic rectitude's disdain of banjos

and pointless failed attempts to rhyme
at the end of a line. The thing about heights
does not acknowledge hollow logs
as legitimate receptacles of supine intention

even in the face of canine inflected
interpersonal animus. Claiming
again insists devious courses come up
but can't find its way to resolve ripples

and waves. Heights don't figure there unless
falling makes a splash and error
as by-the-short-hair bondage imposition
of compulsory dollar day attendance

is left hunting for a space to leave
the car. Having left it anyway is
another possibility. Then the mirror
shatters, and whatever error is the name

that follows it, the pieces and joy
constituting unacceptable humming
bird equivocations by the side of vast
bodies of unresolved ripples and waves.

The light of feathers is in it exuding
wet evasions and undisciplined
sentence's predilection for sloppy
junctions and wobbly dado joints. There's

no way around it. When the hollow log
gets up and takes you in its arms, it's sweet
to kick your heels and holler about how
simply word for word follows past the end.

Canto 63 – Devious courses

The sudden penetration into passages unmarked
on existing skies is not much more than
any easy trick can manage given stacked
decks and rising water. Luck of the draw

will indicate inexorable foundling
destinies trick cards can't rejig into known
outcome's pot. And water up to your nose
is a sure sign. Interpretations

warble when faced with implacable
insistence on sense as a number
of proceeding stars with gifts of story
laden motion. The treasure is in

formidable deviations from ecliptical
assumptions of stable circuits through paths
deemed real. In the distance, sounds of plaintive
cows plodding through the final poems

resemble lonesome whippoorwills and other
figures from the land of broken hearts. They
think the way home is at the end of a
sentence in which long time gets them there for

dinner. Then the stars tilt and all hell
breaks loose. Once out, it changes its name
and begins agitating for unsecured
loans and randomly distributed

alibis widely perceived with unalloyed
suspicion among general indications
of national self-fulfillment. That's
a different kind of hell including

where you stand, the scenic view spreading
erratically toward its many points
of interest, each more tenebrous
than obscure references to ecliptical

deviations suggest. Other hells lurk beyond
acceptable shopping strategies, *une
des forms séduissante du diable*
dancing its funny dance on the table in Walt's

place. Ignore the fact that hope tends
to make you stupid and the theme provokes
fear unless introduced to promiscuous
democracies of sound, "d" doing it hard

with "e" till some new vowel catches its
tone in luxuriant transgressions leading
home into dark alley's necessary
rearrangement of corrosive vistas.

Canto 64 – Hoochy koochy equivocations

*"Therefore Nature changes all food into living bodies, and
from them brings forth all the feelings of animals, very
much in the same way she expands dry sticks into flames
and turns them all into fire."*
— Lucretius, *De rerum natura*

There's no way it wouldn't come back
to damp evocations of sweet, slapping
meat. Stellar bursts of subcutaneous

thinking demand it as irrevocable
determination of orientation toward tree
voices and fluid syllables sibylline

brush with stone. Slap may rhyme
with distances necessary for any fallacy
to slip from light to light, but entering

the difference is only human. If
the feather shines, let there be light and count your
less than precise iterations as fortunate

interregnums. Getting there is not
the point, it's just what happens in spite
of perverse proclivities to follow

gentle slopes into harbours of uncertain
wet intimacies associated
with flammable feelings translation

from comestible. Such a variant
geography, the earth given to sensual
discriminations and unwarranted

deviations into fiery delight
are a constitutional beyond amended
pedal motivations and hollowed out

verbal insulations. Discovering that
past the end of the world is a real
doozy, leaving personal flotation

devices to sink or swim as reveries
of okeanos encounters up the ante
in lingering metaphors from previous

deviations. The view is tremendous
but confused by uninvited elements
insistent disruption of compositions'

tendency to rule out homophonic
disasters. Dark stars enter the fray
unexpectedly awash in the feelings

of animals as they flicker among
the thought of sticks and the heat harboured
in brittle interiors. Sliding

along its breaking, it's rising belly
of moon swollen flame is the sudden
thinking of its unchained lexicon.

Canto 65 – *Obscure and nebulous stars of the human mind*

". . . language will kill you if you give it an inch . . ."
– Gilbert Sorrentino

Occult matters of dubious intent
linger in mapped skies deviant left-over's
Bronx cheer at exterior ballistic's

one damn thing after another. The mill
grinding out star's stories of again's
maelstrom yields unnecessary's

crucial determination. That and obscure
prophetic imprecations will get you
lined up and ready for any

sudden stellar slippage. Knowing where
you are is half the game, though untidy
implications unfold in unseemly

coordinates indicating vicinities
known to harbor perpendicular
penetrations often shunted

into positions involving bars of dubious
intent behind which unusual assignations
leave the Vanishing Point, unexpectedly

back in town, not knowing where to park
its cute little tush. Nebular resolutions
invoke moronic associations though you

wouldn't know it if they saw you. They're sneaky
like that, stars slipping across millennial clicks
doling out aeonic offerings

in portents of inundation and avuncular
termination. To be is a lost
art when war is let out to the lowest

bidder. The tilt is then perceptible
from a certain depth perpendicular
to the ecliptic, especially if

the sun has just stained the sky umber releasing
aubades from their cages. Their flutter
attends a new rhythm resembling water

on stone when the wind picks up scattering
measures over broken multiphonic
stellar excrescences. In tender light

not to be fails to notice the water
at its neck and happily launches another
armed intervention in defense of hilltop

cities' while liberty's interminable
exody follows the hint of new
constellations into delicious cacophonies.

Canto 66 – Restless forms of passage

"Remember, there is no bottom in the sum of things."
– Lucretius, *De rerum natura*

Shoveling white is a good indicator
of precipitous passages through virtually
realized intervention eruptions, white

generally indicating not so much absence
as around the corner. Passages come
and go, unlike Wellington's perennial

cut, butt against stony face then up
again at interrupted top and running
straight and true through heart of uses

specific to prevention of errors
intrusion and perpendicular
penetration's dolomite dreams. Having

got there once is no sure thing when all that's
offered is signed, sealed, and cheesed up
in singular opportunities

of a social nature. The sum of things
coagulates when you insist on
indicating your true feelings looking

very like a cat exiting from a box
full of water. Puzzled by sound
of distant cows, it searches the sky

for signs of who popped the top and what
happened to all the others riding
the wave. The cows are abuzz with wanton

indications of engorged probability
in anticipation of climactic home
coming. When it does, collective sighs

reach for the memory of a smoke. The cat
shakes itself and proceeds into a grin
fades as time contracts and stellar indices

reform in shapes dangle in night begging
for some interloping rhythms to shimmy
across the bony dark rendering

inaccessible into thinking's barely
incomprehensible zig zag flash
across logic's ejaculation, anticipating

arrivals' recalling departures' suspended
sonority straining between till it gives
way leaving nothing humming sweet somethings

in the ear of today's bent proclivities
toward deviant pockets of surprised
but resilient Walden formations.

BOOK 12

OH YEAH!

"Entrapment is this society's / Sole activity,
I whispered / and only laughter /
can blow it to rags."
– Ed Dorn

Canto 67 – Setting up camp

"I am thought, therefore I jam."

Forget your city on hill, high and fine
with a stick up its butt and just go
figure out where to put the damn tent

given the rise of ground and proximity
of that tangled stand of spruce to the fire
pit. The path to the lake may constitute

it. Think of it as blue, a blue constitution
playing out embraces of occupation's
sweet invention. It could be in mountains

the average trip to school saw, or Wednesday
night prayer meeting's insurmountable
hoot factored into itinerant

exclamations of oh yeah resound
in gallivanting paths through explications
of earth. You still have to get to the can so it's best

if paths avoid overwrought extenuations
though meandering encounters in blue
have been known to lead to surprising turns

of morning. The rhythm usually
indicates precarious precipitates'
constitutional inquiry into

thoughts of what is already way past
junctions of where trailing along behind
demanding formations of home

replete with cows, hooves on the table,
sprawling on the chesterfield, ploughing
through the fridge while loping interjects

sunny anthems and hot lead whizzes.
Coming home while being as not coming
home is the trick, a calling beyond not

indifferent. It indicates wavering
interstices which broken haunts with flinching
resolve. The end in sight is not the end

of exclamations victorious
salvational prospects claim
to complete penetrations of intertwined

proclamations, declarations and addresses.
The remains from that stumbles back to the fire
in time for stars and marshmallows, ready

to pack it up when the sun rises and head
off leaving suddenly empty oars stuck
in the mud searching for signs of a new day job.

Canto 68 – Hot diggity dog

"Chord changes? Listen, sweetie."
– Duke Ellington

The diggity suggests probability
wiggles in paradisiacal vision's unsure
formulation of emerging ecstasis
circulations. The next word remains

the next word while the hoot in that amplifies
sonorous deployment of transmogrified
rebound modulations emanate
from stony gullets. Dancing

tongues help, tripping the same light fandango
previous skies undertook with such
passion, skipping stones across still water
in the mouth of anticipation. The next

word attends to the transformation of stones
into foundations of castles in the air
of unexpected expanses. Such heady
extrapolations of atmospheric

disturbances sometimes invokes paroxysms
of hope inspired claims to hilltop beatitudes
unable to regulate convulsive
yelps of lingering sanctity tingling

from shore to shining shore. Then you just
have to sing your heart out as if Jerusalem's
floor plan was nothing so much as a breach
in the exception leading to exophoric

postcedent contingencies. Party time's
chrono-declensions of diggity dogs
exceptional claims for authority
as they emerge in obligatory

graceless nomos contractions reeking
of demands for footnotes. Singing your heart
into knots of blatantly undocumented
dictum arrangements then constitutes

a dream of remarriage, as if conjunctions
of unexpected billy club conversations
and inaugural illusions of born again
temptation might yield a further language

after the end finally gets off its high
horse and steps into forgotten joys
of gravy. Vast reclaimed tracts of jelly roll
terrain breed in seams left exposed

by evaporating self contracted glacial
expressions. The abrupt pools of this
metamorphosis flash with light tasting
the flick of stones across its tongue.

Canto 69 – Improving the nick of time

"For words are not thoughts we have but ideas in things,
and the poet must attend not to what he means to say but
to what he says means."
— Robert Duncan, *The H.D. Book*

Long lost nations of attention awaiting
constitutional interventions
may be confused with boxed cats riding
probability waves through newly

evoked temporal vibratory
apparitions when the cows come home
and the hot lead whizzes. It looks kind of like
the last place, but it sounds different

when the wind comes up raising the waters
to a certain pitch of agitation
speaks obliquely of former encounters
in strange sentences' nick. Even into

the breach doesn't render its endless
resounding in passing away. It leaves
no other room, no other shot at unwritten
cataphoric inclinations to disperse

the time that remains in unthinkable
aeons of chronogenetic funk spurts.
Post-axial points of poultry consumption
jubilation break into the time we our

selves are, *the only time we have* to eat
that chicken *as not eating* in reveries
of dizzy openings into ordinary
moments. Meager differences constitute

no final thought of the end as it
hovers between intricacies of repetitious
fulfillment. Let the cows eat cake, let them
dodge hot lead in the light of further

intimations of Razz and Tootie's
reunion after the long disparate
night. Let the moment split open spilling
wet red seeds into its lap. Then the party

really starts. Each time ticks and wiggles
and boogies to some intimate explication
proceeding in spite of magisterial
images of *Finito*, dazed eyes searching the distance

for a vanished point. Having been
there all along is no excuse for ignoring
all those dimensional breaches into
other festivities whose refusal

to stop evading next leads the whole rock
pile moment stripped of further undulations
signifying industrious adherence
to no nonsense temporal management

into proliferating viral chronos
contagions morphing into the nick's
unannounced appearance looking a lot
like Jimmy Stewart holding open the door.

Canto 70 – Excursions in unknowable worlds

"We do not commonly remark that it is, after all, always the first person speaking."
   – Henry David Thoreau

The usual begins and then just keeps
looking a lot like uninterrupted
instigations of trivial epiphanies
in pursuit of occasions suitable

for hoochy koochy equivocations'
inestimable first person exclamations
coming hard on the heels of sudden
penetralia. Oval interiors

are no place for a serious sentence
to start unless inhabited by
limitless signs of potential egress
especially in circumstances hobbled

by undeclared assumptions of bovine
directional rectitude. Giddy
abbreviations of temporal extension
clog the works with unprecedented

densities of variegated
passages anticipating distant
pasts to come in simple sentence's
sudden cruciform retrogradation

providing plenty of opportunities
for illegal temporal gatherings
where the law attempting to bust polly
wolly doodle bursts of atavistic

laughter reformed into a word juiced
post-prophetic stumble through the jungle

finds itself hung up to dry in the surge
of stuttering annunciation hoots.

Then unknowable's chronic metric
disabling function delivers goods
in exogenous mouthsfull of cold
earth dribbling real efficacy down

surprised restoration of *dictum/
factum* to skies of uncertain blues. Polly
wolly doodle nails it, if only in respect
to diggety function's defense against

anti-riparian requirements
for footnotes establishing wolly's
verbal authenticity and citations
demonstrating its provenance. Leaving

citations to bite the dust of pink guitar
wastelands and avant garde rock pile brain locks
Tootie just moves on to *fairy fey*
recalling the first person speaking.

Canto 71 – More hippy bullshit

"When you get right down to it / said Alpha to Omega /
where will the whole thing end?"
    – James Broughton, *High Kukus*

Getting to Room 203 through corridors
of nothing more substantial than
riparian eruptions in the face
of hostile building codes is unthinkable

when standards for most harmonious
resolutions lie within already
arranged reservations recognized by better
establishments. Stacked trout streams

remain an embarrassment in most god
fearing hotels claiming no-nonsense self
explications as blueprints for career
oriented adjustments of spatio

temporal irregularities into halls
of well-planned asset backed expansion
dissolves in rhythmic constellations
of Pliny's tripped out harmonic spherical

vibratory annunciation. That's way
too much fun to haul within the bounds
of good taste's reasonable rejection
of too young's dark sloe-eyed heat across room's

obligatory gratuitous spatial
contractions. Win big and go boldly leap out
into the night vertiginous flashing
constitutional contingencies in lieu

of contextual degradations, or
perhaps within its arms. A new day
of perplexing embraces in strange joints
introduces an excess of suspense

leaves the end wriggling to get its wits
stacked up neatly and ready for sale.
The trout leave in disgust, muttering long
passages from Huckleberry Finn into clenched

fins. Going to hell then becomes
the baboon rump of new dispensation's
unavoidable imperative to pay
attention to what matters in a time

of universal entrapment arranged
in long parallel rows of shelves stacked
with similar drugs guaranteed to smooth out
whatever variations might disrupt

laminar chronos lockdown. The end is nigh
continues to adorn wavering ontic
antics as shadow determinations tangle
with spasmodic telic ejaculates.

Canto 72 – Jelly roll funk declarations

"I want to be the guy whose armpit sounds like a bagpipe."
– Victor Coleman

What's been found hasn't been lost any more
than articulating registers yield self
evident inalienability in the course
of sudden jamming. Then loudly inclined
terminal extensions serve no other
purpose than exclamatory announcement.

Let the cows have it is one announcement
too many if you adhere to more
beyond occasional yields of other
wise expected manifestations of self
confirming lyric introspection inclined
toward redemptive climaxes in the course

of temporal paralysis. Of course
is the yield, holding any announcement
to barn door closures. Though otherwise inclined
chicken pies look on in attitudes more
akin to incremental shifts of self
decentered crow's nest insight than other

views allow. Armpit revelations of other
tonalities denied in any approved course
of studies indicate independent self
abdication can lead to an announcement
of unparalleled lucidity. What's more
the clamour remains largely inclined

downward or at least outward as inclined
is often wont to do. Then surprised other
returns as meat music, or even more
curious, a post-messianic bagpipe course
available in certain hoot announcement
configurations of fortuitous self

encounter. Petrified remains of self
induced falls into positions inclined ·
toward auto-erotic announcements
give it up to chord breaches into other
places mainly known through devious light course
eruptions into what it says means more.

An end in hand is better than more self
gratified terminal shapely course inclined
allows. There's always another announcement.

TERMINUS

Colophon

Manufactured in an edition of 500 copies by BookThug
in the fall of 2010. Distributed in Canada by the Literary
Press Group: www.lpg.ca. Distributed in the United States
by Small Press Distribution: www.spdbooks.org. Shop on-
line at www.bookthug.ca

BOOK
PRODUCTION
WAR ECONOMY
STANDARD